2600
Phrases
<u>for</u> Effective
Performance
Reviews

2600
Phrases
<u>for</u> Effective
Performance
Reviews
Ready-to-Use Words and Phrases
That Really Get Results

Paul Falcone

American Management Association
New York • Atlanta • Brussels • Chicago • Mexico City • San Francisco
Shanghai • Tokyo • Toronto • Washington, D.C.

Library of Congress Cataloging-in-Publication Data

Falcone, Paul.
2600 phrases for effective performance reviews : ready-to-use words
and phrases that really get results / Paul Falcone.
   p. cm.
   ISBN-10: 0-8144-7282-6
   ISBN-13: 978-0-8144-7282-8
   1. Employees, Rating of—Handbooks, manuals, etc. 2. Performance
standards—Handbooks, manuals, etc. I. Title: 2,600 phrases for
effective performance reviews. II. Title: Two thousand six hundred
phrases for effective performance reviews. III. Title.
   HF5549.5.R3F35   2005
   658.3'125—dc22

2004028328

Printing Number

20 19 18 17 16

Contents

CONTENTS

CONTENTS

CONTENTS

Introduction:
How to Use This Book in Order to
Save Time and Write Compelling
Performance Appraisals

I f you've purchased this book, you're serious about strengthening your written communication skills and developing
your subordinates. The truth of the matter is that most performance reviews in corporate America are drafted without
much thought and are submitted well after the deadline—not
much of a motivational tool for workers longing for appreciation for a job well done. Yet taking the time to formally ap-
praise employees' performance once a year has much more
significance than many managers realize.

In poll after poll, workers rank pay fourth or fifth on the
list of critical workplace factors—well below the critical areas
of open communication and recognition for a job well done.
American management teams fail to recognize the critical importance of ongoing feedback and staff development in employee retention matters—even when there are scarce dollars
available for merit increase pools. The optimal leadership
style provides ongoing feedback day in and day out on a regular and predictable basis. The best people managers realize
that by shifting responsibility for employee performance evaluations back to their staff members, they take themselves out
of the role of unilateral decision maker and disciplinarian and
place themselves into the role of career mentor and coach.

In addition, managers who stand out among their peers recognize that the Development section of any performance appraisal is the most critical piece of the process because it constructs a blueprint for employee growth and learning. The learning curve is indeed the glue that binds people to companies. Despite small merit increase pools or opportunities for vertical promotion available in any company at any particular time, satisfied employees will perform at their best and remain loyal when they feel connected, sense that they make a difference at work, and add critical skills and experiences to their resumes.

They say that people "join companies and leave managers." It's also said that the difference between an active job seeker and a passive job seeker is one bad day in the office. If your most respected critic were to objectively evaluate your leadership abilities and staff development skills, how do you feel you would rank if were evaluated according to the following criteria:

➤ How effective are you at delegating to and motivating your staff?

➤ How consistent are you in putting their career and development needs above your own in a goodwill attempt to help them build their resumes and prepare for the next step in progression in their careers—at your company or elsewhere?

➤ How well do you address performance achievements and problems day in and day out so that subordinates understand what is expected of them and how success is measured in your group?

The annual performance appraisal process is the once-a-year validation that someone is making a positive difference—that their contributions over 365 days of work are formally recognized and celebrated. Yet, too many managers fill in annual appraisal forms in a perfunctory fashion, looking at the process as a bothersome, yet mandatory task. Enlightened managers, on the other hand, make their jobs much easier by delegating appropriately, listening attentively, and having fun at work. It's not that hard to transition to "enlightened management" status: All it takes is a willingness to rethink your role in your company, your influence over those you supervise, and your ability to bring out the best in others by motivating them to reach beyond their comfort zone.

Remember that motivation is internal. You're not responsible for motivating your staff, per se; people are responsible for motivating themselves. You are, however, responsible for creating a work environment in which people can motivate themselves and find new ways of reinventing their work in light of your company's changing needs. To that end, this book will serve as a handy time saver, a narrative assistant, and an insightful guide into new ways of recognizing and rewarding performance.

How to Use This Book

It is often the case that managers avoid or delay written communication tasks that may appear to be confrontational. Similar to a book I've written called *101 Sample Write-Ups for Documenting Employee Performance Problems: A Guide to Progressive Discipline and Termination*, this book's key purpose is to help you find the right words and descriptive phrases to communicate your thoughts and perceptions in a concrete manner for specific situations.

In Part I, we'll address the most commonly rated performance factors, or "core competencies," that a majority of companies use to assess their workers. Included among the core competencies are the topics of "managerial style" and "personal style"—often the most difficult issues to describe in an annual performance review. The phrases in these sections fit a variety of interpersonal and managerial styles, commitment levels, pace, need for structure, emotional intelligence, and ability to prioritize and juggle multiple tasks. Refer to these sections any time you have a difficult time finding the right words to describe an individual's preferences, inclinations, peculiarities, or other outstanding features. You might just find a special way of phrasing something that, up to now, you've had a hard time identifying and describing in others.

For each of the commonly rated performance factors in Part I, we provide descriptive phrases that can be used to evaluate *historical* performance, organized in two sections:

Meets/Exceeds Expectations
Needs Improvement

For all of the core competencies we also provide a third section called "Goals." This section provides multiple examples of development plans for outlining key areas of *future* growth and learning. These phrases will help you structure your recommendations for employee improvement over the coming review period. As with the two other sections, you could simply use these statements "as is" or customize them for your particular needs.

Simply stated, forward-looking development plans give you a process to prevent future performance problems and to create an environment in which employees could motivate themselves. That, more than anything, will give you peace of mind and turn you into a motivator and coach rather than a unilateral disciplinarian and decision maker. Your employees will benefit too as they're given the freedom and discretion to self-monitor and self-correct in an empowered environment. There's no greater formula for enlightened leadership.

Whereas Part I covers general core competencies, in Part II we address the *functional* components of many common positions in Corporate America, including positions in sales, marketing, finance, legal, human resources, operations, information technology, and manufacturing. It is important to be able to benchmark particular functions and responsibilities that are common in such universal positions, and to address performance expectations for each.

There are four appendixes in the book. Appendixes A and B provide useful lists of high impact verbs and adverbs that will prompt you when finding just the right word tends to escape you. Appendix C is a brief discussion of merit increases and the five-point grading scale. Appendix D is a short index of the titles and roles that appear in this book.

In essence, in this book you have a handy library of practical, ready-to-use phrases that will help you acknowledge outstanding job performance, address substandard work quality, and outline developmental opportunities for your direct reports. In addition to saving time, you'll strengthen your self-confidence and distinguish yourself in writing as a leader and career builder.

The Performance Management Cycle

There are three components of the Performance Management Cycle:

1. Goal setting and planning
2. Ongoing feedback and coaching
3. Appraisal and reward

The annual performance appraisal clearly speaks to the third issue, but appraisal and reward can't be accomplished in a vacuum. That third stage is the culmination resulting from ongoing efforts in the first two stages. The performance management cycle is a continuum leading to a particular resolution in the final (third) step, but all three stages are intrinsically linked to the end result—the performance appraisal and associated merit increase (reward).

Annual performance appraisals are not meant to be a paper chase—a mandatory exercise that creates a snapshot of your impressions as a supervisor about a subordinate's work. Instead, they should be a collaborative effort that builds on open communication and constant feedback. Thus, investing in goal setting should be a two-way communication: Employees who have advanced input into their own career development will typically buy in to the suggestions much more readily than when those goals are imposed from above. And remember, no matter how "perfectly written" these goals are on the actual performance appraisal form, they'll be useless without ongoing communication throughout the review period.

So keep a copy of each of your staff member's annual reviews in your desk, and make sure they do the same. Develop a habit of reviewing the status of performance achievement and skills development on a quarterly basis. You'll find that your business relationships will be focused, you'll never again feel like you're flying blind, and your subordinates will have less of a need for ongoing supervision.

Ten Tips to Maximize Your Performance Appraisal Documentation Skills

Whenever you pull this book down from your bookshelf as you're preparing to write a subordinate's performance review, keep the following rules in mind:

Rule 1: There should be very few surprises in the annual review.
This is a "total recall" document reflecting twelve months of work. If something totally new needs to be surfaced now,

you probably didn't do a thorough enough job communicating with the employee throughout the review period.

So sharing performance concerns for the first time during the performance appraisal should be the exception, not the rule. Still, sometimes it may be necessary to do so, even though that may appear to "blind side" the employee. Nothing is more demotivating than finding out that your overall performance didn't meet company expectations when you thought you were doing fine. Typical complaints sound like this:

"I can't believe my boss. She gave me an overall review score of 2 out of 5, meaning that I didn't meet expectations. It would have been nice if she'd told me some time over the past year that I needed to improve in a particular area. She's always so nicey-nice and perky to your face, and then she stabs you in the back on the annual review. Well, I have a pending meeting with the division president to discuss my supervisor's shortcomings, and this review she gave me will be the first item of discussion."

To avoid such lose-lose situations, whenever you're faced with documenting new issues for the first time in an annual review, acknowledge in writing that the matter hasn't been formally brought to the employee's attention beforehand. For example, "I recognize that we haven't formally discussed . . . , but I felt it appropriate to bring this issue to your attention during this annual performance review because. . . ."

Assuming you have a compelling reason to include brand new information in a document that covers an entire year's performance, this open and honest approach will make your documentation appear to be more objective and evenhanded. More importantly, the employee may perceive the entire matter as ultimately fairer because the disclaimer at least acknowledges that this is new terrain.

Rule 2: Review the employee's prior year performance review(s) before attempting to draft a new appraisal.

Performance reviews aren't meant to be conducted in a vacuum. They only make sense if they logically follow the prior year's performance appraisal notes. Therefore, look to prior reviews for areas of particular strengths, weaknesses, or areas for development. Which areas have improved? Which areas have remained stagnant and in need of further development? What's the overall performance trend when comparing this year to last year?

Rule 3: Understand how documentation can be used against your company if composed the wrong way.

Here's a special consideration: When employees are terminated for cause and bring wrongful termination actions against prior companies, judges and arbitrators look to the consistency in a company's written communication in order to justify the termination and determine which party prevails. This *written record* is typically found in the form of written warnings and annual performance reviews, laid out side by side on a table as exhibits. But which one is more important in an arbitrator's eyes: the annual review or the written warning?

Generally speaking, the annual appraisal is given more weight in legal deliberations because it covers an entire year's work. A written warning, in comparison, could simply be the result of one bad day in the office or a short-term string of thoughtless acts or omissions. Think of it this way: A written warning typically functions to *break the chain* of positive performance evaluations that's been documented over a number of years. Still, the annual appraisal is generally viewed as the "anchor" document that evidences the company's formal communication record with its worker.

In comparison, the written warning serves to reestablish and redirect the company's written communication record by placing an individual on notice that *failure to provide immediate and sustained improvement may result in further disciplinary action, up to and including dismissal.* Disciplinary consequences written this way clearly state that an individual's position is in serious jeopardy of being lost. It would subsequently be very difficult for plaintiff attorneys to argue that their client (your ex-employee) was denied workplace due process because the individual couldn't discern—based on your company's formal communication record—how serious the situation had become.

The question you have to ask, of course, is whether one written warning or multiple warnings will be necessary to justify a termination. That can only be answered on a case by case basis, depending on an individual's tenure, historical performance record, and protected category status. Remember, however, that you have a lot more discretion to terminate or issue a final written warning for a first-time "conduct" offense (like theft or insubordination) than for a "performance" infraction (like substandard work quality). In the case of performance infractions, you'll typically be expected to provide workers with all the steps of progressive discipline typically accorded under your company's policies and past practices, which could include written and final written warnings as well as suspensions, in some cases.

However, if written warnings are subsequently followed by a positive annual performance review showing that the employee has improved and now meets company expectations, then that positive performance evaluation will, in essence, nullify the written warning issued during the review period. So if you have any remote hesitations about an individual's ability to make it in your department or company in the upcoming year because of his subpar job performance or inappropriate workplace conduct, document it! You should grade the individual as "not meeting expectations" in the "Overall Score" section at the end of the performance appraisal form.

Otherwise, the positive record that you create today will make it harder to terminate the individual tomorrow.

Rule 4: Performance reviews are absolute, not relative.

Too many unsuspecting, yet good-hearted managers feel that they've given an employee a *real* message regarding their substandard performance by assigning them lower grades than everyone else on the team. If the other four employees in your unit received "exceeds expectations" scores (for example, 5 out of 5), and this particular individual received only a "meets expectations" score (for example, 3 out of 5), shouldn't she realize that she's performing poorly?

Absolutely not! If the company deems a 3 an acceptable score, then the employee *hears* that she's met expectations. In a court of law, that individual employee may state that she realized that she scored lower than everyone else in the department or that she had no idea what scores the others received. In either case, her lawyer's argument will simply state that she had no idea that her job was in jeopardy because her overall score was acceptable.

The lesson here is simple: If the *overall score* for the performance period shows that the individual is not meeting company expectations, then your communication record will remain consistent and incontestable in its intent. On the contrary, trying to hang your hat on the "message" that one person received the lowest overall score in the unit is no defense to a wrongful termination charge. A jury most likely would not sustain your logic that the employee had cause to believe that she was heading down the road to termination.

Likewise, most performance appraisal forms have nine or ten individual categories in addition to the "Overall Score" at the end. Substandard scores in individual categories will certainly help your case if you're forced to defend a termination, but in and of themselves, they may not be an absolute defense. Instead, be sure to give the individual a failing

"Overall Score" at the end of the appraisal form to reflect unacceptable performance for the entire review period.

Rule 5: It's okay to give an A.

Do you remember those college professors who never gave A's? It seemed that no matter how hard you worked or how much extra credit you turned in, they were simply implacable: An A was little more than a lofty dream.

It shouldn't work that way in the workplace. Saying thank you for a job well done and recognizing special achievements should be a matter of practice, not a matter of exception. It's perfectly acceptable to write at the conclusion of an appraisal:

Patty, thank you for your ongoing contributions and continued hard work over the past year. You've made our department a better place by your willingness to assume additional responsibilities, your friendly customer service, and by the care you put into everything you do. Keep up the excellent work, and remain a role model for your peers. I'm proud of you and very appreciative of all you've done.

Again, your merit pool may only be 2 percent, or maybe you have no merit pool at all this year. The overall score on the review shouldn't be lowered because you have a smaller merit pool than you'd ideally like to have. What's important is the written message: Those parting words in the annual review, now made into a formal company record, will have an incredible impact on your employee's sense of job satisfaction and self-worth. And think what a gift you'll have given her to share with family and friends at home as well as perspective employers in years to come.

Of course, you should also be a bit cautious about being too flowery in your accolades and compliments. Should that employee later fall from grace and you terminate the individual for cause, your stellar recommendations from prior years may be enlarged and placed before a jury as evidence of the individual's worth and work ethic.

Rule 6: Don't give everyone A's!

If you routinely give all of your direct reports the highest overall grade rankings, you're probably doing something wrong. It's possible to say that at one particular point in your career, every individual member on your team may be the best worker you've ever had the joy of supervising. Maybe you've got the best line-up of staff members in your entire industry. Reality, though, is probably not quite as optimistic: Managers who award A's to everyone on their team often have the problem of distinguishing between genuine superior performance and overall good work. They also often wish to avoid the confrontation that comes with providing more down to earth, albeit realistic performance scores.

The solution is pretty simple: Rank order your staff in terms of who is your most critical contributor versus who probably would make the least difference if she resigned tomorrow. Your superstar would be a 5; your "least stellar" worker, who still performs at a very acceptable level, would be a 3. Your other staff members will probably fall into the 4 category.

Think of it another way: You're not doing your subordinates any favors if you continuously give them 5s. Agree together on areas for growth and learning and push them to develop their technical skills and formal education by attending discipline-specific workshops and conferences. It's a more honest appraisal methodology, and a 5 will really be something to strive for.

If you've only given 5s in the past but want to give more 4s and 3s this year, simply hold a staff meeting in advance of the performance appraisal meetings and let your subordinates know that you'll be evaluating everyone differently this year. State that although you've typically given higher grades to the group in the past, you want to work on customizing each appraisal this year in terms of objective feedback and development plans. That means the overall scores may be a bit lower, but the value of the entire process, especially the development plan, will increase, and that's to everyone's benefit.

Rule 7: Whenever possible, shift the responsibility for evaluating performance back to your employees.

The reason most employees receive their evaluations late is because supervisors don't have the time to collect the data necessary to write a good review. In addition, since relaying negative news can be confrontational (and we all know that the path of least resistance is avoidance), many supervisors postpone documenting subpar performance for fear of making matters worse with the staff.

You'll find (much to your surprise!) that many employees will appreciate the opportunity to bring to your attention their perceptions of how they've done, what they plan to do, and how you could help. And that automatically puts you in the role of career mentor and coach—not unilateral decision maker and disciplinarian. You'll also learn that the majority of workers will be harder on themselves than you would have ever been. That should take some of the stress off of you in terms of having to surface negative information.

It works this way: About a week before you need to draft your staff appraisals, instruct your direct reports to address their overall performance in three critical areas:

1. Address your overall performance track record for this review period. Specifically address your achievements that have resulted in increased revenues, reduced expenses, or saved time. Why is XYZ Company a better place for your having worked here? How have you had to reinvent your job in light of our department's changing needs? And how

would you grade yourself in terms of work quality, reliability, interpersonal communication, and technical skills?

2. In what area(s) do you feel you need additional support, structure, or direction? Specifically, where can I, as your supervisor, provide you with additional support in terms of acquiring new skills, strengthening your overall performance, and preparing you for your next move in career progression?

3. What are your performance goals for the next year? What are the measurable outcomes so that we'll know that you'll have reached those goals?

Once you receive their initial feedback, you could then go on to draft your own staff appraisal. By allowing employees to take the first stab at outlining their goals and achievements, you'll automatically capture what they feel are their most significant issues. You'll be reminded of the achievements they've made throughout the year, and you'll be in a much better position to draft a comprehensive and objective annual report.

Expect an "emotional involvement rate" of 20–70–10 in this exercise, as follows:

➤ 20 percent of your staff will love this exercise and provide you with all the bells and whistles—productivity graphs, cost savings spreadsheets, and copies of letters of recommendation they've received from customers throughout the review period. (This is the key target group for the exercise.)

➤ 70 percent will do an adequate job in engaging themselves in the self-review process; however, their answers may be somewhat superficial or unsubstantiated.

➤ 10 percent may refuse to participate: They might argue that it's your job to evaluate them and not theirs. But then

again, that tells you a lot about their motivation and entitlement mentality, doesn't it? Maybe their own refusal to
participate should be incorporated into the narrative of
the annual review as evidence of their overall work ethic.

On the other hand, you may naturally fear confrontation by
allowing employees to initiate the process and have first say.
For example, if you feel that one particular employee is a
subpar performer, but that individual may think he's the best
thing since sliced bread, then you're sure to invite conflict,
right? Wrong! Remember, *you* write the actual review. This
pre-review draft is not the actual appraisal form that will end
up in the employee's personnel file.

And if it turns out that you both have very different perceptions of the individual's contributions, it's okay to disagree.
This will provide you a key opportunity to open up the lines of
communication regarding reasons for the differences in your
perceptions. After all, if you simply roll over the individual in
the annual review process like a Sherman Tank with a one-
sided diatribe, you'll only initiate a paper war with a stark
rebuttal. Talk first, then write. If you both agree to disagree,
then so be it. In the end, you'll keep control of the entire
process, your authority will remain intact, and you'll initiate
a dialog to reach a mutual ground. If the employee follows
your review with a rebuttal nonetheless, it will likely be mil-
der and "less attacking" if there have been open discussions
before anything was committed to writing.

One final thought: Some employees will request formal
feedback on a more regular basis than once per year. (You
know who they are.) Consider formally reviewing them twice
a year or even possibly once per quarter by shifting the responsibility for data collection and initial review back to
them. In essence, they'll do all the legwork, and you'll create
an environment in which they could motivate themselves. It
requires a minimal time investment on your part, and you'll

find that they'll spread the good news about your enlightened management style with their peers. Objective feedback on a consistent basis is what it's all about.

Rule 8: Don't formally document or otherwise discuss the merit (salary) increase during the performance review process.

If you document, "I believe Janet should receive a 5 percent merit increase this year based on her performance" or raise this issue verbally during the performance appraisal meeting, expect Janet to focus on salary from that point forward. Whether she challenges your overall merit increase recommendation or simply spends the next few minutes of the meeting trying to determine how much that 5 percent uplift will impact her biweekly paycheck, the focus will shift away from performance. Since this is a *performance* review as opposed to a salary review meeting, keep merit increase discussions out of the meeting. They will only weaken your message and lessen your ability to bring about change in the individual's performance levels over the upcoming review period.

Rule 9: You have the right to add disciplinary language to an annual performance review, turning it, in effect, into a written warning.

When managers confirm ongoing substandard performance issues in an annual appraisal, they often mistakenly believe that they must then wait an additional 30 or 60 days before initiating a formal written warning. In essence, the two steps may be combined to hasten the progressive discipline process.

Occasionally, it may be appropriate to add disciplinary language to the performance review itself, thereby turning the substandard performance appraisal into a formal written warning. Your narrative might look like this:

In addition to documenting that your overall performance for this review period does not meet company expectations, this annual ap-

praisal will also serve as a formal written warning. Failure to demon-strate immediate and sustained improvement may result in further disciplinary action up to and including dismissal.

You'll thereby have established a written record of communicating that the individual's employment is in serious jeopardy of being lost.

Of course, this suggestion could seem a bit extreme, depending on your company's policies and past practices, or a collective bargaining agreement may preclude such aggressive actions. Still, depending on the nature of the infraction as well as the employee's tenure with the company and status as a protected worker, it could certainly be worth pursuing. When in doubt, speak with your HR department or qualified outside counsel, especially if this will be the first time your company will have engaged in this practice of combining annual reviews with formal written warnings.

Rule 10: Follow a few narrative-writing tips that will help you consistently strengthen your overall message.

First, be sure to avoid writing anything that could be interpreted as discriminatory. You may not document or reference anything protected by privacy or employee protection laws. For example, writing "Michael, you are performing well since you began your new medication to combat depression, and I encourage you to continue" could very well violate the protections afforded by the Americans with Disabilities Act if the individual is later denied a promotion or terminated for cause. Similarly, if you reference an individual's age, ethnicity, sexual or gender orientation, religious beliefs, medical history, or any other categories protected under Title VII of the Civil Rights Act or other state worker protection laws, then your own documentation could be used against you in a court of law.

Similarly, if an employee was on a leave of absence for a

significant part of the review period, simply document that "Michael was on an approved leave of absence from May 10 to August 8" and leave it at that. The reason for the leave (pregnancy, workers comp injury, stress leave) is superfluous and should not be included as part of the formal record established by the performance review. It follows that all performance appraisals should be reviewed in advance by your HR or Legal departments before they are shared with your employees to ensure, among other things, that no discriminatory language exists.

Second, avoid the term *attitude* in your formal business communication with your subordinates. "Attitude" is a very subjective judgment that courts will typically dismiss because it is often associated with a mere difference of opinion or a personality conflict. Instead, be sure to describe the objective behaviors that create a negative perception of the employee in others' eyes. Only behaviors and actions that can be observed and documented belong in work place discussions and may be presented as evidence in court.

For example, replace an admonition like this:

"As we have discussed throughout the year, you have received many complaints regarding your attitude. *You need to demonstrate immediate improvement in this area."*

with something concrete like this:

"Peggy received a written warning on January 14 for raising her voice in anger and for using profane language directed at a coworker. The disciplinary warning specifically stated that if she ever again lost control of her temper, used profane language in the workplace, or demonstrated behavior that could be perceived as hostile or threatening, further disciplinary action up to and including termination could result."

Third, use the phrase "For example" at least three times in an individual performance appraisal. Managers often make sweeping comments about perceptions without documenting the factual circumstances that justify their points of view. You could therefore easily turn a perception statement like "Your planning and organizational skills are satisfactory, but you sometimes require additional assistance in this area" into something more concrete and instructional for the employee by including an example.

Fourth, use the terminology "needs improvement" cautiously in your narrative writing, as it may not convey the message you intend. The examples in our book are structured according to the following two criteria:

Meets/Exceeds Expectations
Needs Improvement

Note, though, that these are categories only for ease of use. In reality, stating that performance or behavior "needs improvement" is not the same as stating that *it does not meet company standards* or is *unsatisfactory*. Similarly, documenting that "Richard has been *spoken to* regarding excessive absenteeism and tardiness" does not convey that his performance was unacceptable. Don't assume that the employee understood (or a jury would agree) that just because you *spoke about* performance which *needed improvement,* it was assumed to be substandard. Instead, clearly document when performance is unacceptable, unsatisfactory, or fails to meet standards.

Fifth, you should document the efforts you've made to help the employee meet performance standards throughout the review period. When writing annual performance appraisals, for example, you should include the fact that you gave the employee a copy of the attendance policy, paid for her to attend a workshop on dealing with interpersonal conflict in the work place, or encouraged her to take an accounting course at a local college. Such documentation will serve as evidence that you acted responsibly by attempting to proactively rehabilitate the worker.

Finally, when documenting core competency or technical issues, expand your basic ideas by employing a *"by . . ."* format, like this:

✧ Regularly places support staff in positions of leadership *by* appointing them subject matter experts in particular technical areas or by selecting them for workshop/seminar facilitator roles.

✧ Assumes responsibility for areas beyond his immediate control *by* preparing the monthly income statement, the comparative balance sheet, and overall general ledger maintenance.

✧ Has done very little to maintain and advance his technical knowledge and skills *by* upgrading his software skills, attending educational workshops, establishing a professional network of peers, or participating in professional societies.

✧ Masters all phases of the project development life cycle *by* identifying and documenting requirements, technical processes and procedures, test documentation, and environment and deployment plans.

✧ Successfully negotiates salary offers and preempts counteroffer possibilities *by* "pre-closing" and proactively engaging finalist candidates in discussions about their future career development.

✧ Ensures that newly learned skills are repeated and enforced *by* following up with 30, 60, and 90 day quizzes and questionnaires.

Similarly, when documenting future development goals, you could easily strengthen the clarity of your message by applying the *"I expect you to . . . by . . ."* format. For example, it would be simple to turn a statement like:

"In the upcoming review period, you must improve your client relations skills and better utilize your time."

into a more instructional, future-oriented statement by applying the *"I expect you to . . . by . . ."* structure, which would look like this:

> "I expect you to improve your client relations skills *by* following up with customers within two hours of their initial calls, *by* meeting them in their offices rather than asking them to come to yours, and *by* maintaining weekly contact regarding the status of their work order processing."

Of course, the examples themselves will easily stand on their own without the "by" predicate. Still, this structure should help to remind you to complete your thoughts and provide appropriate examples for your statements. Selectively added to the annual review at strategic points, it will add critical mass to the statements that you make and justify your perceptions. It will likewise help you clearly outline your performance expectations and how they will be concretely measured. Clarity in your written message will not only protect your company from potential outside legal challenges; it will help build a shared sense of open communication, a greater sense of partnership, and increased accountability with your workers.

A final tip to readers:

A book like this will necessarily contain overlap. When you look up a title relating to *management*, be sure to look under both Parts I and II in the text. Part I contains sections on the core competencies of "Leadership," "Managerial Style," and "Supervision," which will surely help you crystallize your ideas. Part II, in comparison, contains *specific* managerial positions in the functional areas of manufacturing, operations, and sales and marketing. Be sure to cross-reference other sections of the book whenever possible.

PERFORMANCE APPRAISAL PHRASES FOR CORE COMPETENCIES AND COMMONLY RATED PERFORMANCE FACTORS

Adaptability and Change Management Skills

Meets/Exceeds Expectations

- ✧ Readily identifies more efficient ways of doing business
- ✧ Maintains composure when faced with stressful situations
- ✧ Calms those around her by keeping them focused on the end goal
- ✧ Rapidly adapts to changes in the nature of his assignments
- ✧ Welcomes constructive criticism
- ✧ Shows initiative when having to redefine the way she is performing a task
- ✧ Remains a proponent of change
- ✧ Goes with the flow and adapts readily to any changes in circumstances
- ✧ Welcomes change as an opportunity
- ✧ Is a versatile team player capable of handling diverse assignments
- ✧ Demonstrates a keen ability to multi-task and juggle competing priorities
- ✧ Quickly adapts to deviation from a pre-planned schedule and course of action

Needs Improvement

✧ Appears reluctant to embrace last-minute changes in direction

✧ Strictly adheres to only those job duties outlined in her job description

✧ Does not "roll with the punches" effectively

✧ Demonstrates a tendency to resist even minor changes

✧ Postpones or delays training and implementation of new programs

✧ Remains unwilling to carry out tasks that are "below him"

✧ Does not excel at independent, research-based activities

✧ Avoids covering for others in the department when needed

✧ Becomes frustrated when faced with unexpected changes in plans

✧ Tends to resist or resent new work assignments

✧ Often raises her voice and "lashes out" at her peers when things don't go as planned

✧ Demonstrates a time-clock mentality

✧ Becomes flustered when interrupted or asked to deviate from a fixed schedule

Adaptability and Change Management Goals

✧ Become more willing to take on duties not outlined in your job description

✧ Learn to deal with unexpected changes in plans

✧ Become more adaptable to any changes in your work assignments

✧ Look for ways of using new technologies in order to increase your efficiency

✧ Support organizational restructuring efforts in a constructive manner

Attendance and Punctuality (Reliability)

Meets/Exceeds Expectations

✧ Is fully reliable in terms of attendance and punctuality
✧ Arrives at meetings on time and well prepared
✧ Attained perfect attendance over the review period
✧ Had only two unplanned absences during the entire review period
✧ Begins each day refreshed and eager to face new challenges head on
✧ Never misses work without gaining the appropriate advance approvals
✧ Regularly arranges for back-up temporary support when absent
✧ Complies with all company standards of performance and conduct
✧ Meets all attendance and tardiness standards
✧ Is always willing to work long hours on little or no notice
✧ Remains at her desk throughout the majority of the workday
✧ Begins each day refreshed and eager to face new challenges
✧ Schedules vacation requests well in advance

- Begins meetings on time and ends them on schedule
- Is consistently dependable and conscientious
- Ensures that subordinates strictly adhere to rest and meal periods
- Completes assignments accurately and meets deadlines as promised

Needs Improvement

- Fails to assume responsibility for his actions
- Does not meet standards for attendance and punctuality
- Fails to follow appropriate call-in procedures during absence
- Frequently arrives late to meetings while insisting that his subordinates arrive on time
- Demonstrates a lack of respect for others' time by arriving late at meetings
- Allows cell phone calls to interrupt business meetings with staff and clients
- Generates an excessive number of personal phone calls throughout the day
- Spends excessive time handling personal matters on the Internet
- Received written warnings for excessive unscheduled absenteeism
- Comes and goes as he pleases, citing his "exempt" status
- Does not consistently obtain advance approval for arriving late at work
- Has again used the maximum number of sick days allowed
- Tends to wander from his desk, leaving office phones uncovered

✧ Does not return phone calls and e-mails in a timely manner
✧ Continuously patterns his sick days around regularly scheduled time off

Attendance and Punctuality Goals

✧ Develop a reputation for reliability and excellence in all that you do
✧ Arrive at the office on time and ready to begin work by your scheduled start time
✧ Speak with me in person (not by leaving voicemail message) when you need time off
✧ Strictly adhere to all break and meal periods
✧ Plan to arrive on time at all meetings out of respect for others' time
✧ Strive to attain perfect attendance
✧ Provide medical documentation for any leaves in excess of five days
✧ Arrange for back-up temporary support any time you are going to be out
✧ Check with me before you leave at night to see if I need help with anything
✧ Schedule your vacation requests well in advance of proposed leave dates
✧ Re-read the company policy regarding punctuality and adhere to its guidelines
✧ Do not allow outside telephone calls to interrupt your work
✧ Avoid taking sick days up to the policy maximum
✧ Do not wander away from your desk without informing me of your whereabouts
✧ Avoid "patterning" your sick days around your weekends and holidays

Communication and Cooperation

Meets/Exceeds Expectations

✧ Regularly asks for immediate feedback to ensure understanding

✧ Remains open-minded and willing to entertain others' ideas

✧ Communicates clearly with customers who do not speak English fluently

✧ Cultivates a culture of openness in information sharing

✧ Builds consensus

✧ Regularly solicits constructive feedback

✧ Asks well-thought-out and well-prepared questions

✧ Stands out among her peers as a public speaker and corporate spokesperson

✧ Explains complicated issues clearly and succinctly

✧ Demonstrates candor and a sense of humor in all business dealings

✧ Possesses a knack for summarizing and communicating end results

✧ Effectively shares highlights of conferences and workshops with her peers

✧ Speaks persuasively and convincingly

✧ Is not afraid to say "I don't know" or "I'll check on that and get back you"

✧ Demonstrates a willingness to hear others out before reaching a decision
✧ Always makes others feel comfortable to participate and share their opinions
✧ Allows subordinates to share their achievements at weekly staff meetings
✧ Creates an inclusive work environment
✧ Always makes others feel welcome to drop by her office or interrupt her
✧ Acts as a calming influence when faced with anger or resentment
✧ Holds weekly staff meetings to ensure open communication
✧ Provides timely feedback and follow-up
✧ Regularly conducts postmortems on failed deals and learns from his mistakes
✧ Builds strong working relationships with other internal departments
✧ Provides ongoing feedback in a spirit of constructive criticism
✧ Encourages open communication, cooperation, and the sharing of knowledge

Needs Improvement

✧ Creates a territorial atmosphere
✧ Readily attributes blame to others
✧ Regularly complains of a lack of necessary resources to perform effectively
✧ Has difficulty distinguishing clearly between macro issues and micro details
✧ Tends to "foxhole" and isolate himself

✧ Refuses to commit her staff's time to other departments when asked

✧ Has difficulty boiling down complex issues into their component parts

✧ Fails to communicate bad news upward

✧ Asks questions for questions' sake

✧ Engages in shouting matches

✧ Uses defamatory, derogatory language to humiliate staff members

✧ Delays passing along bad news for fear of potential confrontation

✧ Is too wordy to communicate a clear and compelling message

✧ Remains reluctant to provide subordinates with constructive feedback

✧ Fails to take disciplinary actions when subordinates fail to meet expectations

✧ Appears unable or unwilling to say *no* to any request

✧ Prefers that others deliver bad news, even if it's clearly her responsibility

✧ Makes others feel intimidated and uncomfortable when they ask for help

Communication and Cooperation Goals

✧ Cultivate a culture of openness and information sharing

✧ Build consensus via shared decision-making

✧ Ensure that your direct reports are informed of each others' activities

✧ Readily admit if you're not sure of an answer

✧ Be conscious of your body language at all times

✧ Manage others' expectations appropriately

✧ Clearly state up front if you will not be able to deliver as requested

✧ Readily share information and resources to support business objectives

✧ Build trust through regular, open, and honest communication

✧ Listen and respond to others appropriately using a respectful tone

✧ Answer incoming telephone lines within two rings

✧ Say *yes* when you mean *yes* and *no* when you mean *no*

✧ Do not leave callers on hold for more than 30 seconds

✧ Proactively feed information upwards to keep management well informed

✧ Stop others immediately from speaking to you in a derogatory tone

✧ Refrain from using comments like "It's not in my job description"

✧ Be careful not to appear overwhelmed or anxious about the workload

✧ Don't treat coworkers who interrupt you as if they're inconveniencing you

✧ Always deliver bad news quickly and tactfully

✧ Avoid blaming or censuring others publicly

✧ Nod your head to communicate that you are actively listening

Creativity and Innovation

Meets/Exceeds Expectations

- ✧ Thinks outside the box when faced with challenging situations
- ✧ Funnels creative recommendations into practical applications
- ✧ Fosters a spirit of creative collaboration by giving teams a common focus
- ✧ Created a reporting system that is now used throughout the company
- ✧ Skillfully changes direction when faced with new information
- ✧ Solved a long-standing software glitch through a creative workaround
- ✧ Is always willing to take a fresh look at policies and practices
- ✧ Thinks of imaginative alternatives when confronted with obstacles
- ✧ Questions common practices in order to identify better ways of doing things
- ✧ Displays originality and contributes fresh ideas
- ✧ Encourages coworkers to be inventive and to take appropriate risks
- ✧ Makes ongoing suggestions to improve operations

Needs Improvement

❖ Demonstrates little innovation or creativity
❖ Tends to process information in a rote manner
❖ Is slow to adjust his work in light of clients' changing needs
❖ Fails to give credit to subordinates who generate new ideas and solutions
❖ Often gets too "creative" in changing established procedures without approval
❖ Appears unwilling to take creative chances
❖ Fails to tap the creative potential of peers and subordinates
❖ Only initiates courses of action that have guaranteed outcomes
❖ Does not seek creative alternatives to conventional practices
❖ Is reluctant to explore new approaches or alternatives

Creativity and Innovation Goals

❖ Seek out new ideas from others
❖ Consistently acknowledge staff members who generate new ideas
❖ Obtain approval before you change established procedures
❖ Encourage creativity and independent thought among subordinates
❖ Be willing to "think out of the box" when solving difficult problems

Customer Satisfaction

Meets/Exceeds Expectations

- ✧ Works very well with clients as well as all staff members
- ✧ Has a very warm rapport with everyone she comes in contact with
- ✧ Follows up with clients to ensure no one feels forgotten or lost in the process
- ✧ Clearly enjoys the "people" aspect of his position
- ✧ Consistently answers the phone with a smile and a friendly hello
- ✧ Readily admits when she doesn't know the answer to a particular query
- ✧ Outlines the steps that she will take to resolve a problem
- ✧ Receives ongoing positive feedback from clients—both verbally and in writing
- ✧ Has become the "go to guy" for clients who seek his advice to solve problems
- ✧ Excels at providing timely feedback to even the most difficult customers
- ✧ Consistently gains necessary approvals and authorizations
- ✧ Is able easily to switch from English to Spanish and back again
- ✧ Is an empathetic and focused listener

- Skillfully overcomes customers' objections
- Deals with challenging customers without becoming aggressive
- Has developed a loyal customer base and a high rate of repeat business
- Enjoys identifying "out-of-the-box" solutions for clients with special needs
- Skillfully manages all but the most challenging customer situations
- Knows when to ask for additional support from team management
- Is able to redefine the customer service process to meet clients' changing needs
- Overcomes objections in a logical and conversational fashion

Needs Improvement

- Receives ongoing substandard customer satisfaction scores
- Does not manage customer expectations by explaining reasons for delays
- Has difficulty saying *no* or tactfully telling customers that they must wait their turn
- Refers too many customer queries to management for final resolution
- Has received numerous customer complaints for failing to follow up as promised
- Cannot yet demonstrate sufficient knowledge of company products
- Misses opportunities for cross-selling and overcoming initial objections

- Is unwilling to adapt his tone and personality to fit a particular caller's style
- Argues and uses inflammatory language with customers
- Becomes frustrated when customers ask too many questions
- Displays sarcasm and alienates those looking for help
- Demonstrates condescending behavior when dealing with overly demanding callers
- Has little patience for customers with "dumb questions"

Customer Satisfaction Goals

- Demonstrate total commitment to outstanding customer service
- Always exhibit creativity and flexibility in solving customers' problems
- Share information and resources readily
- Make sure that clients understand that you're on their side
- Never appear to talk down to or to patronize customers
- Exceed customers' expectations by providing timely feedback and follow-up
- Quickly address problems even with the most demanding customers
- Effectively prioritize your workload based on your customers' needs
- Share only as much information with a client as is necessary
- Refrain from speaking poorly of the competition
- Never permit customers to treat you disrespectfully
- Involve management whenever customers behave inappropriately

- ✧ Proactively inform customers of pending delays
- ✧ Never use pressure to close a deal or to unduly influence a customer's decision
- ✧ Always put the client's needs above your own
- ✧ Provide objective and timely advice to customers
- ✧ Tactfully tell customers *no* when their demands or expectations cannot be met
- ✧ Follow up with customers after the conclusion of a sale

Diversity Orientation

Meets/Exceeds Expectations

✧ Appreciates the diverse nature of the company's workforce

✧ Supports the company's diversity mission and outreach initiatives

✧ Encourages individuality and respect of others' personal differences

✧ Creates a work environment where staff can express their opinions openly

✧ Welcomes new ideas and ways of looking at things

✧ Appreciates the importance of workforce diversity

✧ Welcomes differing points of view

✧ Always treats subordinates and superiors with respect

✧ Builds an environment of trust and openness in information sharing

✧ Proactively identifies labor pools that could provide more diverse candidates

✧ Reinforces the advantages of attracting and retaining a diverse workforce

✧ Views diversity as a strategic business initiative

✧ Recognizes the value of having our workforce reflect our diverse customer base

Needs Improvement

✧ Has created a perception of potential unfairness among the ranks

✧ Has publicly made "politically incorrect" and thoughtless statements

✧ Has forwarded inappropriate e-mails that were offensive to others

✧ Makes no effort to create teams that reflect the diverse workforce

✧ Tends to make judgments based on stereotypes

✧ Has received complaints regarding his "cliquishness" with certain subordinates

✧ Tends to use objectionable language to or about people who are "different"

✧ Has made numerous off-the-cuff remarks that others found offensive

✧ Is reluctant to confront inappropriate workplace behavior

✧ Makes no effort to understand cultural values different from her own

Diversity Orientation Goals

✧ Recognize diversity as a critical business issue

✧ Create a positive and inclusive work environment

✧ Strive to attract and retain a diverse workforce

✧ View diversity as a way of meeting our public mission and corporate goals

✧ Encourage new ideas from people with different orientations

✧ Recognize each individual's unique contribution to the team

- ✧ Treat others with respect and expect them to respond in kind
- ✧ Actively recruit and develop a diverse team
- ✧ Incorporate different styles, skills, and backgrounds in the people you hire
- ✧ Provide ongoing career guidance and coaching to all subordinates equally
- ✧ Encourage collaboration and teamwork at all times
- ✧ Use the diversity outreach program to better deal with a diverse customer base
- ✧ Recognize that everyone brings unique attributes and experiences to the table
- ✧ Foster a sense of collaboration and joint problem solving

Goal and Objective Setting

Meets/Exceeds Expectations

✧ Sets attainable goals that are compatible with staff capabilities

✧ Ensures that stakeholders are informed of their responsibilities and deadlines

✧ Clearly communicates specific objectives and end results to team members

✧ Ensures that staff members understand their accountabilities and responsibilities

✧ Establishes challenging standards that stretch the limits of his staff's abilities

✧ Reviews results with staff on a monthly and quarterly basis

✧ Proactively shares results regarding her progress with her supervisors

✧ Provides opportunities for others to rotate into key roles of responsibility

✧ Establishes concrete performance standards

✧ Holds himself accountable for meeting performance goals and objectives

✧ Sets clear and measurable performance goals and objectives

✧ Determines measurable outcomes to ensure that goals are reached

✧ Sets aggressive targets to meet both short- and long-term business needs

Needs Improvement

✧ Is inconsistent in making assignments and setting objectives
✧ Puts too much pressure on herself to exceed objectives
✧ Fails to prepare appropriate back-up plans or alternative resources
✧ Provides vague instruction when staff needs more specific direction
✧ Sets unreasonably high performance goals
✧ Does not communicate in advance that a deadline will not be met
✧ Leaves management feeling as if it is "flying blind" about progress
✧ Fails to attain goals because of reluctance to delegate to her subordinates
✧ Makes excuses and blames others when goals are not achieved
✧ Is unwilling to assume responsibility for missed deadlines or error-prone work
✧ Allows distractions to get in the way of reaching goals

Goal- and Objective-Setting Goals

✧ Clearly communicate progress toward goals
✧ Employ metrics to track your productivity and efficiency
✧ Set attainable performance goals for your staff
✧ Meet regularly with your staff to review results
✧ Be as specific as possible when giving directions to your staff

Initiative

Meets/Exceeds Expectations

✧ Consistently pursues her own professional development

✧ Regularly takes on responsibility for areas beyond his basic duties

✧ Assists other departments with special projects that arise

✧ Reinvents processes and redefines the workflow in light of changing needs

✧ Has successfully automated portions of a manual process

✧ Is willing to work whatever hours are necessary in order to get the job done

✧ Approaches clients with a can-do attitude

✧ Looks for creative solutions around traditional obstacles

✧ Assumes new responsibilities whenever the opportunity arises

✧ Researches outside sources and best practices to improve her knowledge

✧ Does not hesitate to question ways we've always done business

✧ Is typically the first in line to put newly acquired training tools to the test

✧ Requires little or no direction in performing day-to-day responsibilities

✦ Looks for what needs to be done rather than waiting to be told

✦ Assumes a leadership role whenever an appropriate occasion arises

✦ Asks for additional responsibilities whenever possible

✦ Is not afraid to make errors

Needs Improvement

✦ Tends to demonstrate a "time clock mentality"

✦ Fails to assume responsibilities beyond the basic, written job description

✦ Often says, "That's not how we did this at my last company"

✦ Discourages others from assuming broader job responsibilities

✦ Resists training and continues to "do things the old way"

✦ Lacks the confidence necessary to bring about change in the department

✦ Offers few creative suggestions or alternatives

✦ Fails to pursue out-of-the-ordinary solutions for customers with special needs

✦ Resists applying newly learned skills

✦ Sometimes takes initiative too far by overstepping his authority

✦ Fails to take advantage of available external training options

✦ Always sticks to the tried and true

✦ Resists picking up his pace when the tempo of the office increases

✦ Has trouble doing her work without ongoing direction from management

Initiative Goals

- ✧ Look for ways of adding value to your role
- ✧ Reconfigure your work in light of our department's changing needs
- ✧ Don't wait for work to come to you—go out and find it
- ✧ Ask not what your company can do for you—ask what you can do for your company
- ✧ Research matters thoroughly before asking for help
- ✧ Keep a notebook handy with shortcuts and rules of thumb to save time
- ✧ Make yourself a valuable business partner to your clients
- ✧ Identify and fulfill customers' needs on a proactive basis
- ✧ Demonstrate interest in professional development opportunities
- ✧ When things are slow in our area, ask for more work
- ✧ Look for ways you can contribute beyond your current job description
- ✧ Keep abreast of trends and changes in our business
- ✧ Attend two outside workshops to further your professional development
- ✧ Take advantage of our tuition reimbursement program to complete your degree
- ✧ Identify ways to fill any skills gap that may exist in your resume
- ✧ Self-identify areas for development and growth
- ✧ Strive to become more independent in your role

Job Knowledge

Meets/Exceeds Expectations

- ✧ Demonstrates a thorough knowledge of his key responsibilities
- ✧ Is technically adept at all facets of her work
- ✧ Regularly keeps me abreast of key developments and decisions in her area
- ✧ Serves as our resident expert for administration and training
- ✧ His knowledge about our company goes well beyond his area of responsibility
- ✧ Regularly translates product features into benefits
- ✧ Takes a "strategic business partner approach" to his work
- ✧ Learns about other departments' key initiatives
- ✧ Maintains an extensive network of industry associates
- ✧ Is keenly aware of key players at competitor firms
- ✧ Documents common processes and steps in an internal troubleshooting guide
- ✧ Shares her knowledge with her peers in the department
- ✧ Spearheads seminars to cross-train others
- ✧ Keeps abreast of trends and changes in her field

Needs Improvement

- Has little awareness of our competitors
- Fails to demonstrate appropriate forecasting ability
- Has difficulty locating information when needed
- Repetitively asks basic questions that she should know the answers to
- Is not adequately versed in key aspects of his work
- Produces more errors than someone with her experience should
- Fails to demonstrate mastery of basic concepts in his area of responsibility
- Produces substandard and untimely work product
- Depends too readily on specific instruction from supervisors
- Fails to think issues through to their logical conclusions

Job Knowledge Goals

- Continuously develop the breath and depth of your skills
- Gain a deeper understanding of your clients' expectations
- Develop goals based on your understanding of business priorities
- Enroll in an extension course to enhance your skills and knowledge
- Engage in rotational job shadowing exercises to learn others' roles
- Become an "issue spotter" by learning what issues are concerning your clients
- Research our competitors

- Study our annual report to understand relevant trends and forecasts
- Review your job description to ensure you understand all aspects of your job
- Find out what you need to know without asking repetitive questions
- Become our department's "go to" person for special projects
- Strive to stand out among your peers in terms of job knowledge
- Actively transfer your knowledge to junior staffers
- Initiate departmental lunch-and-learn seminars to cross-train your staff
- Sign up for internal training courses and independent study

Judgment and Decision Making

Meets/Exceeds Expectations

✧ Displays sound judgment when deciding among multiple alternatives

✧ Reaches conclusive decisions after researching alternatives thoroughly

✧ Remains an impartial and objective evaluator of facts

✧ Doesn't allow his emotions to cloud his business judgment

✧ Is decisive even in times of tight deadlines and budget constraints

✧ Encourages her direct reports to have equal input into decision making

✧ Remains calm in times of crisis

✧ Avoids unnecessarily hasty decisions

✧ Never appears to "sweat the details," no matter how great the pressure

✧ Appears confident and persuasive when defending his decisions

✧ Is always able to identify the core issues at hand

✧ Makes confident decisions once she has gathered the facts

✧ Provides swift solutions to routine questions

✧ Demonstrates a unique focus on results

✧ Knows which problems require immediate solutions and which can wait

❖ Knows when to call in additional corporate support
❖ Is able to outline the pros and cons of alternative courses of action

Needs Improvement

❖ Makes decisions without weighing alternative courses of action
❖ Displays a conventional, unimaginative approach toward solving problems
❖ Allows direct reports to make too many decisions without prior approval
❖ Gets bogged down by "analysis paralysis" when forced to make decisions
❖ Complains openly about business problems to all who will listen
❖ Tends to use a "my way or the highway" decision-making approach
❖ Avoids confrontation and delays decisions that could upset others
❖ Does not consistently think through alternatives
❖ Often responds "I haven't thought of that" when asked basic questions
❖ Makes no independent decisions without management's advance blessing
❖ Focuses more on avoiding mistakes than on thinking of creative solutions
❖ Practices risk avoidance more than risk management
❖ Makes inappropriate comments in public
❖ Shares confidential information about the private affairs of coworkers
❖ Tends to exacerbate rather than improve tense situations

✦ Makes too many big decisions without management approval

Judgment and Decision-Making Goals

✦ Use business knowledge to make timely and effective decisions
✦ Demonstrate sound judgment under pressure
✦ Use appropriate and relevant information when making decisions
✦ Don't get bogged down by "analysis paralysis"
✦ Avoid making snap decisions without getting buy-in from key stakeholders
✦ Avoid shifting responsibility for decisions to others
✦ Remain decisive and steadfast once you have communicated a plan of action
✦ Avoid sugarcoating disappointing news
✦ Never exceed your authority when speaking on behalf of the company
✦ Ask for advance permission for decisions that do not adhere to company policy
✦ Wait to hear both sides of a story before making a decision
✦ Give more decision-making responsibility to your subordinates
✦ Always assume responsibility for decisions gone wrong
✦ Make decisions that not only reflect policy but also past practice
✦ Make more cost-effective decisions in line with the budget
✦ Remain open to all sides of an argument before making a decision

Leadership

Meets/Exceeds Expectations

- ✧ Leads by example
- ✧ Places the needs of her staff above her own
- ✧ Provides adequate structure, direction, and feedback to subordinates
- ✧ Ensures open communication and staff camaraderie
- ✧ Recognizes and rewards staff achievements
- ✧ Encourages staff to assume responsibility for their actions
- ✧ Listens actively
- ✧ Allocates his resources appropriately in the face of competing demands
- ✧ Creates a culture of mutual trust and caring
- ✧ Channels strategic vision into concrete plans of action
- ✧ Consistently earns respect from subordinates
- ✧ Holds herself accountable for staff performance
- ✧ Readily shares information and develops staff by delegating to their strengths
- ✧ Provides strategic vision of future goals and objectives
- ✧ Develops plans for achieving goals and objectives
- ✧ Always puts others' needs before his own
- ✧ Readily assumes responsibility for her actions
- ✧ Successfully manages the tactical steps needed to push a project forward

✧ Staff would "follow him into battle" because he's decisive and loyal
✧ Takes appropriate risks and encourages others to do so
✧ Makes high probability decisions even when she doesn't have all the facts
✧ Demonstrates high standards of ethics and fairness

Needs Improvement

✧ Over-analyzes problems when swift decision making is needed
✧ Confuses subordinates by sending mixed signals about goals and priorities
✧ Fails to maintain confidential information
✧ Fails to plan for future needs
✧ Often flouts corporate policy and appears to march to his own drummer
✧ Is ill prepared to debate and defend an intended course of action
✧ Rarely shows appreciation for a job well done
✧ Demonstrates an entitlement mentality
✧ Appears unwilling to accommodate subordinates' needs
✧ Does not yet trust his instincts to lead and motivate others
✧ Sets unreasonably high expectations for himself and others
✧ Uses his position to dominate and intimidate others
✧ Fails to generate enthusiasm for new projects and initiatives
✧ Does not recognize or reward subordinates' achievements

✧ "Plays favorites" and does not treat people fairly
✧ Blames others for errors and failure to meet goals

Leadership Goals

✧ Strive to build alliances whenever the opportunity arises
✧ Identify and partner with key business stakeholders
✧ Build relationships within and across departments
✧ Engender trust and respect among your teammates
✧ Build support for ideas through persuasion and consensus building
✧ Make others feel welcome to seek your advice and counsel
✧ Learn others' preferences and amend your style to accommodate their needs
✧ Appreciate that things can be accomplished in many different ways
✧ Encourage and support work-life balance for yourself and others
✧ Volunteer for leadership opportunities in industry and charity events
✧ Build trust through regular, open, and honest communication
✧ Regularly assume responsibility for new projects and programs
✧ Be willing to incur risk
✧ Create a learning environment
✧ Make it safe for subordinates to make mistakes and volunteer new ideas
✧ Coach people to prepare for their next move in career progression
✧ Lead work teams and task forces with authority and self-assurance

- ❖ Ensure alignment with corporate goals through teamwork and communication
- ❖ Inspire others to follow your example
- ❖ Inspire a high level of trust from others
- ❖ Create an environment where employees feel valued, respected, and trusted

Listening Skills

➤ ◀

Meets/Exceeds Expectations

✧ Demonstrates active and focused listening skills

✧ Allows others to complete their thoughts before replying

✧ Makes sure others "feel heard" and feel free to express their opinions

✧ Has mastered the skill of "mirroring back" what she hears others saying

✧ Always attempts to understand others' points of view

✧ Maintains eye contact and nods her head to demonstrate attention and agreement

✧ Listens objectively and with an open mind

✧ Waits one full second after someone finishes speaking before rebutting

✧ Genuinely empathizes with others who have differing points of view

✧ Actively elicits feedback even from those with opposing views

✧ Always demonstrates a sincere interest in others' points of view

✧ Asks appropriate questions when unsure of instructions or directives

✧ Accurately interprets what was said the first time

⬥ Allows others to share their thoughts and experiences without critique
⬥ Only needs to be told once
⬥ Follows directions and instructions carefully

Needs Improvement

⬥ Asks questions that show that he is not actively listening
⬥ Gets distracted by her own ideas and loses track of a conversation
⬥ Only hears what he wants to hear
⬥ Interrupts and speaks over peers
⬥ Always tries to finish others' thoughts for them
⬥ Has developed a reputation for "having to have the last word"
⬥ Stops listening if he feels attacked or challenged
⬥ Constantly interrupts others amid thought
⬥ Loses the ability to objectively hear what is being said when criticized
⬥ Readily dismisses others' ideas when she wants to change topics

Listening Goals

⬥ Become a more effective listener
⬥ Demonstrate active listening skills as a sign of respect for others
⬥ Understand how verbal interruptions damage interpersonal communication
⬥ Listen for what's being implied as well as what's actually being said

✧ Avoid interrupting others

✧ Improve the quality of your work relationships by listening more attentively

✧ Regularly maintain eye contact with speakers

✧ Count to two after others finish speaking before initiating a response

✧ Practice mirroring back what you hear others say

✧ Listen objectively even during heated negotiations

✧ Immediately ask questions when you don't understand something

✧ Don't talk out of turn

✧ Ensure that others don't have to repeat themselves

Managerial Style

Meets/Exceeds Expectations

- ❖ Creates an inclusive work environment
- ❖ Recognizes each person's uniqueness
- ❖ Models the "natural leader" paradigm
- ❖ Communicates a compelling and inspired vision
- ❖ Always projects the right mix of enthusiasm, strength, and energy
- ❖ Treats people with respect and expect them to respond in kind
- ❖ Is a calming influence in a storm
- ❖ Always provides constructive feedback
- ❖ Assigns tasks fairly and evenly
- ❖ Maintains open and ongoing communication with her staff
- ❖ Knows how to get things done through both formal and informal channels
- ❖ Effectively marshals resources
- ❖ Sets very high expectations of himself and his staff
- ❖ Encourages and rewards team performance
- ❖ Compensates for her subordinates' weaknesses and limitations
- ❖ Is looked to for direction in a crisis

- Brings out the best in people
- Supports fair and equal treatment
- Enjoys working with and learning from others
- Deals with problems head on rather than letting them fester
- Is consistently fair in parceling out assignments
- Has established rewards and recognition that reinforce desired outcomes
- Always recognizes individual needs and skills when delegating work

Needs Improvement

- Fails to set and monitor goals, targets, and mileposts
- Has developed a reputation as a nonconformist
- Tends to instill fear in subordinates
- Typifies a "live and let live" management style that borders on apathy
- Comes from the "information is power" school, where little information is shared
- Is too quick to replace subordinates rather than to grow and develop them
- Rarely celebrates or shares successes
- Fails to adjust her approach for different audiences and situations
- Provides too much negative and too little positive feedback
- Avoids confrontation at all costs
- Deals with staff in a heavy-handed and intimidating way
- Pulls rank and overpowers others
- Remains overly optimistic about staff's abilities
- Comes across as distant and aloof

- Is known for having an argumentative and intimidating disposition
- Tends to over-delegate and not do enough of the work herself
- Is too focused on internal operations rather than the needs of customers
- Concentrates on the development of few at the expense of many
- Tends to give subordinates too much room for excuses
- Often "hogs the work," leaving others with little to do and her with too much
- Openly challenges and confronts others who express contrary opinions
- Avoids face-to-face interaction and relies on e-mail instead

Managerial Style Goals

- Work through conflict and ensure productive resolution
- Confront and address inappropriate behavior immediately
- Build trust at every opportunity
- Develop a more collegial relationship with your direct reports
- Make others feel welcome to seek your advice and counsel
- Practice random acts of kindness with subordinates
- "Catch" people being good
- Demonstrate effective decision-making and problem-solving skills
- Discourage subordinates from unfounded speculation about private matters
- Remain consistent in your interpretation and application of company policy

- ❖ Avoid feeding the "corporate grapevine" with unfounded facts or rumors
- ❖ Communicate in advance any potential deviations from standard procedures
- ❖ Motivate others to be their best and strive to bring out the best in them
- ❖ Maintain confidentiality of private or sensitive information
- ❖ Regularly ask others for and openly provide feedback
- ❖ Create a culture of open information sharing and increased accountability
- ❖ Seek public speaking opportunities to develop your presentation skills
- ❖ Make it safe to volunteer differing points of view

Oral and Written Expression

Meets/Exceeds Expectations

✧ Speaks clearly and confidently without hesitation
✧ Addresses others in an open fashion
✧ Is totally at ease when addressing a large audience
✧ Allows others to complete their thoughts before countering their arguments
✧ Acknowledges others' points of view
✧ Never has a bad thing to say about anyone
✧ Always has a smile on her face
✧ Articulates her thoughts clearly and logically
✧ Constructs compelling arguments
✧ Is effective at saying no respectfully but firmly
✧ Uses clear and simple language
✧ Her correspondence never gets bogged down in unnecessary detail
✧ Is careful not to speak over her audience
✧ Composes correspondence that is brief, well structured, and error free
✧ Creates useful spreadsheets for capturing and filtering large amounts of data
✧ Documents complex ideas in a user-friendly fashion
✧ Keeps all written memos to one page

- Uses bulleted formats that clearly capture an issue's salient points
- Writes clear and persuasive memos
- Creates and uses compelling PowerPoint slides to amplify presentation
- Debates skillfully and convincingly and "holds his own" very well

Needs Improvement

- Speaks too quickly and appears to ramble at times
- Quickly loses her audience
- Suffers from a fear of public speaking
- Sometimes "whines" and weakens the value of his spoken message
- Commits confidential information to e-mail
- Fails to synthesize key points in his writing
- Allows excessive narratives to distract from his written message
- Fails to use spell check and other electronic tools
- Publishes memos with spelling and grammatical errors
- Tends not to stick to the point in her writing
- Does not check memos for errors before distributing them
- Tends to back down and acquiesce whenever openly challenged
- Hesitates to verbally defend her stated position
- Writes excessively long memos that make it difficult to crystallize key points
- Overuses boldface and exclamation marks in his memos
- Lacks a basic mastery of business writing techniques
- Fails to record edits and changes in the redlining process

Oral and Written Expression Goals

- Write to express, not to impress
- Write succinctly
- Use no more than three bullets to capture the essence of your message
- Purchase and read a book on grammar to help you keep memos error free
- Begin your memos with your conclusion or ultimate recommendation
- Consistently use the spell-check feature before sending e-mails to others
- Structure your ideas neatly into paragraphs
- Use simple language that is clear and concise
- Write in a natural, conversational style
- Employ executive summaries to present your key points and ideas
- Keep proposals to one page whenever possible
- Don't "shout" when you write by using too many exclamation marks
- Always ask questions to confirm your understanding
- Connect with your audience by walking around the room
- Refrain from using sarcasm
- Never appear to whine or complain about matters beyond your control
- Use a bulleted format to structure e-mail messages succinctly
- Avoid providing too much detail
- Count to two after someone finishes speaking so as not to interrupt them
- Paraphrase what you hear someone saying to confirm your understanding

Organization and Planning Skills

Meets/Exceeds Expectations

✧ Displays excellent organization and planning skills

✧ Takes a methodical and consistent approach toward organizing her work

✧ Locates back-up information quickly

✧ Plans, organizes, and completes tasks in an acceptable time frame

✧ Readily adheres to deadlines and production benchmarks

✧ Maintains a very neat and well-organized working environment

✧ Will not leave to go home at night unless everything is put away in its place

✧ Develops practical alternatives to various "what if" scenarios

✧ Has created a processing system that allows coworkers to step in during his absence

✧ Demonstrates a well-honed ability to forecast potential problems and pitfalls

✧ Always plans tomorrow's goals before he leaves the office

✧ Consistently relies on a PDA to keep fully informed of her calendar

✧ Manages multiple tasks effectively

✧ Documents repetitive tasks

✧ Files documents immediately upon receipt
✧ Is very effective in anticipating bottlenecks
✧ Duly considers the possible outcomes of a particular course of action
✧ Proposes strategies and tactics that are concrete and definitive
✧ Anticipates potential areas of growth for our core product lines
✧ Is highly proficient in anticipating resource needs
✧ Always creates various "what if" scenarios to counter contingencies
✧ Prepares her assignments in a systematic and orderly fashion
✧ Never appears to be overwhelmed by the sheer volume of work

Needs Improvement

✧ Has difficulty planning a course of action without specific instruction
✧ Does not plan ahead
✧ Fails to head off minor problems before they become major impediments
✧ Does not communicate when he requires additional support or assistance
✧ Has difficulty translating theoretical ideas into tactical action plans
✧ Demonstrates a reactive, "management by crisis" style
✧ Has difficulty keeping two steps ahead of his current project load
✧ Gets lost in a myriad of details
✧ Quickly loses sight of the bigger picture

✧ Does not consistently tie up loose ends and wrap up projects cleanly

✧ Fails to plan for and follow through with detail work

✧ Consistently fails to plan for the unexpected

✧ Does not make contingency plans should initial assumptions prove wrong

✧ Tends to over-commit her time

✧ Is inconsistent in tracking incoming statements and records

✧ Fails to consult with other stakeholders when planning a large-scale project

✧ Does not conduct proper needs assessments in the pre-planning stage

✧ Appears overwhelmed and disorganized despite years of tenure in this role

Organization and Planning Goals

✧ Plan your work and work your plan

✧ Become a more effective goal setter

✧ Prepare contingency and alternative plans

✧ Understand and implement the key benefits of organization and planning

✧ Identify and address organizational needs

✧ Rely on a daily planner to block periods of time for particular tasks

✧ Do not over-commit your time or resources

✧ Ensure that you don't allow last-minute interruptions to get in your way

✧ Automate several of the paper-intensive tasks on your desk

✧ Strengthen your forecasting ability

✦ Maintain a workspace that is free and clear of clutter

✦ Dedicate one hour per week to thinning the outstanding reports on your desk

✦ Plan for the appropriate level of resources when undertaking a new project

✦ Avoid scheduling conflicts

✦ Focus on both short- and long-term plans

✦ Don't get discouraged by unexpected delays

✦ Establish both strategic and tactical planning goals

✦ Translate goals into concrete action plans

✦ Always plan for the unexpected

Personal Style

Meets/Exceeds Expectations

✧ Willingly accepts constructive criticism

✧ Always displays a high level of enthusiasm, humor, and spontaneity

✧ Consistently looks for ways of improving performance

✧ Respects others' differences

✧ Encourages openness in information sharing

✧ "Lives to work" rather than "works to live"

✧ Displays a genuine appreciation for her job

✧ Always has a "can do" attitude

✧ Demonstrates a keen eye for detail

✧ Works well in a large bureaucratic system

✧ Always exudes a high level of self-confidence

✧ Respects both the letter and the spirit of company policies

✧ Uses diplomacy and tact in dealing with staff and clients

✧ Likes neatness and order at work

✧ Has a well-deserved reputation for accuracy and completeness

✧ Effectively diffuses high tension situations

✧ Demonstrates selflessness in putting others' needs before his own

✧ Analyzes successes and failures for clues to improvement

- Serves as an excellent source of institutional knowledge
- Builds constructive and supportive relationships with peers
- Does not let personal disagreements interfere with the work at hand
- Asks insightful and penetrating questions
- Exemplifies commitment, discipline, and a solid work ethic
- Demonstrates patience when confronted with organizational shortcomings
- Sees how things can be done rather than why they can't be done
- Uses humor to ease tension
- Is able to acknowledge her own shortcomings
- Goes the extra mile to put others at ease
- Demonstrates a high level of energy, drive, and determination
- Is sought out by others for advice and counsel

Needs Improvement

- Prefers to work alone
- Often uses sarcastic and offensive humor
- Takes rejection too personally
- Is too hard on herself
- Has a reputation for being cynical and moody
- Prefers to keep others at arms' length
- Gets mired in minutia and tedious detail
- Over-relies on his engaging personality rather than substantive work
- Tends to pit individuals against one another
- Engages in rumors and talks behind people's backs
- Doesn't know when to confront and when to hold back

- Takes criticism as a personal affront and becomes very defensive
- Antagonizes others by showing a superior attitude
- Often lets her anger, frustration, and anxiety show
- Tends to be hypercritical of others
- Appears to be stuck in a comfort zone and won't take risk
- Tends to make excuses rather than dealing with problems head on
- Has developed a reputation for being a complainer and whiner
- Has difficulty turning theoretical vision into workable practice
- Gets sidetracked as soon as a more exciting challenge comes along
- Flits from activity to activity without tying up loose ends
- Readily assigns blame to others
- Has a penchant for overcomplicating matters
- Makes inappropriate and offensive comments and gestures
- Often is too free with confidential information
- Lets things fall through the cracks
- Sometimes seeks change for change's sake
- Rationalizes away mistakes

Personal Style Goals

- Become more comfortable dealing with authority
- Always remain in control even in the face of urgent deadlines
- Avoid becoming frustrated by your own or others' shortcomings
- Pick up on social cues and learn to read people accurately

- Learn to say *no* forcefully rather than passing tasks up the line
- Allow others to finish their thoughts before rebutting their arguments
- Become more effective at managing others' expectations
- Never get personally involved in others' conflicts
- Design three development goals that you know you can achieve
- Make conscious effort to "lighten up" your style
- Assume responsibility for a problem rather than blaming others
- Become a more positive influence on coworkers
- Accept the challenge of change in a dynamic environment
- Become more proficient in the use of new technology
- Learn to plan instead of flying by the seat of your pants
- Become more efficient at drafting documents and proposals
- Produce results without getting bogged down in red tape
- Be patient when dealing with crises and chaos
- Pick your battles wisely
- Learn to laugh more
- Be willing to take risks
- Never resent requests to do something outside of your normal duties
- Remain flexible when faced with last-minute changes in plan
- Take constructive criticism in stride and avoid appearing defensive
- Serve as a role model of service and professionalism
- Remain productive and results-oriented
- Model an appropriate sense of urgency
- Practice multitasking rather than performing "one task at a time"

Problem-Solving Skills
and Results Orientation

Meets/Exceeds Expectations

✧ Successfully identifies, analyzes, and solves problems

✧ Approaches problems in a positive manner

✧ Views impediments as solvable challenges

✧ Shows patience in dealing with complex and time-consuming issues

✧ Willingly shares knowledge so that others don't have to reinvent the wheel

✧ Identifies practical solutions

✧ Clearly explains options and solutions to end-users

✧ Breaks down obstacles into their component parts

✧ Resolves issues in a timely manner

✧ Addresses problem issues head on in a proactive fashion

✧ Analyzes possible obstacles in order to identify solutions

✧ Maintains an open dialogue with clients who are having technical problems

✧ Always recommends at least two solutions to every problem

✧ Keeps supervisors apprised of status changes and requests for resources

✧ Is able to diagnose complex problems and reach sustainable solutions

Needs Improvement

✧ Fails to recognize repetitive trends in recurring problems
✧ Becomes unnerved when dealing with demanding customers
✧ Approaches problems in a linear fashion, solving only one matter at a time
✧ Fails to provide multiple solutions or to demonstrate lateral thinking skills
✧ Has difficulty troubleshooting basic user questions
✧ Suffers from information overload when resolving complex tasks
✧ Excessively bothers her peers with questions about basic matters
✧ Sometimes misses the practical first step in diagnosing a problem
✧ Often cannot distinguish between core problems and secondary symptoms
✧ Fails to provide staff with the appropriate amount of structure and direction
✧ Appears overwhelmed when faced with multiple problems
✧ Does not make adequate use of online support tools
✧ Does not seem to learn from past mistakes

Problem-Solving Goals

✧ Learn to anticipate problems in advance
✧ View obstacles as challenging problems that can be solved

- ✧ Be a problem solver rather than a complainer
- ✧ Effectively distinguish between the causes and the symptoms of problems
- ✧ Become adept at juggling multiple priorities under time constraints

Productivity and Volume

Meets/Exceeds Expectations

✧ Consistently meets or exceeds productivity targets
✧ Regularly completes work ahead of schedule
✧ Constantly finds the right balance between volume and quality
✧ Encourages others to exceed our department's monthly goals
✧ Does not sacrifice quality for volume
✧ Is recognized as a consistent top producer
✧ Readily tackles new projects that require a substantial investment of time
✧ Maintains unusually high output
✧ Sustains peak performance
✧ Uses quarterly staff meetings to review annual development goals
✧ Volunteers for assignments beyond normal work hours
✧ Prides himself on his well-deserved reputation as a "volume hound"
✧ Constantly exceeds targeted benchmarks
✧ Employs metrics to measure and maximize her group's productivity
✧ Breaks production records
✧ Generates minimal product returns

* Measures results through established metrics and analytical benchmarks
* Diagnoses problems that impede productivity

Needs Improvement

* Remains inconsistent in reaching monthly performance targets
* Commits excessive input errors
* Experiences a higher than average scrap rate
* Does not consistently meet output benchmarks
* Exhibits only superficial product knowledge
* Lacks troubleshooting abilities
* Does not look beyond her job description for ways to increase productivity
* Fails to encourage cooperation and collaboration from other departments
* Processes a low volume of work relative to her peers
* Continues to make mistakes despite ongoing training efforts
* Has been unable to avoid staff burnout
* Appears sleepy and unfocused throughout the morning

Productivity and Volume Goals

* Increase both the volume and quality of your work
* Overcome internal barriers to productivity
* Learn how to manage frequent interruptions
* Discipline yourself to plan your work and work your plan
* Enhance your overall reliability
* Meet attendance and punctuality goals without exception

- ❖ Promote innovation and creativity in your group
- ❖ Conduct a postmortem of any failed project to learn from mistakes
- ❖ Set monthly goals and track progress on a weekly or daily basis
- ❖ Ensure maximum participation in staff meetings
- ❖ Keep focused whenever unexpected events play havoc with best-laid plans
- ❖ Streamline work processes and increase efficiency
- ❖ Hold weekly meetings to ensure that staff members communicate openly
- ❖ Identify risks before accepting assignments
- ❖ Ensure that you have the necessary manpower and resources in place
- ❖ Gain perspective on any potential productivity deficiencies

Professionalism and Grooming/Appearance

Meets/Exceeds Expectations

- Maintains a professional appearance in dress and manner
- Always has a smile and a friendly "How are you" to share with others
- Represents our company well at all off-site meetings
- Readily adheres to the company dress policy
- Is always direct and honest when dealing with others
- Motivates team members, always leading by example
- Demonstrates professional expertise in all that she does
- Consistently acts within company guidelines
- Makes compelling, organized presentations
- Adheres to a traditional code of honor and respect for others
- Places others' needs before her own
- "Walks the talk"—his actions are always consistent with his word
- Always justifies exceptions to policies and past practices
- Remains calm and focused in high-stress situations
- Welcomes constructive feedback from peers and staff
- Treats people with dignity and respect at all times
- Avoids using inappropriate jargon or idioms

Needs Improvement

✧ Does not project an image of professionalism
✧ Is inconsistent in enforcing company policies and procedures
✧ Is often disrespectful and unfair in dealing with subordinates
✧ Fails to display an acceptable standard of grooming
✧ Is inconsistent in following ethical business practices
✧ Fails to meet personal hygiene standards
✧ Tends to use overly familiar terms like kiddo or buddy
✧ Fails to take steps to strengthen the overall impression she makes
✧ Often arrives at work with uncombed hair and in wrinkled clothes
✧ Has not taken responsibility for his own career development
✧ Lets past differences interfere with her teamwork
✧ Feeds the corporate grapevine with unsubstantiated facts
✧ Fails to pick her battles wisely
✧ Alienates clients by engaging in thoughtless gossip
✧ Challenges others with baseless claims

Professionalism Goals

✧ Establish immediate credibility
✧ Inspire and motivate those around you to perform at their best
✧ Demonstrate vision, ambition, persistence, and a passion to succeed
✧ Project a positive self-image

- ✧ Always exude self-confidence and inspire confidence in others
- ✧ Dress the part in order to create an initial impression of success
- ✧ Display the highest level of personal integrity
- ✧ Demonstrate best practices in all that you do
- ✧ Treat others with dignity and respect at all times
- ✧ Maintain composure and professionalism when faced with crises
- ✧ Support a more inclusive and positive work environment
- ✧ Insist that staff members meet standards of grooming and appearance
- ✧ Maintain confidentiality and respect for others' private affairs
- ✧ Create an image of professionalism and class in all that you do
- ✧ Respect and follow company policies and procedures
- ✧ Treat others with respect and fairness and expect them to respond in kind
- ✧ Follow ethical business practices at all times and tolerate no exceptions

Quality

Meets/Exceeds Expectations

✧ Displays pride in his work
✧ Ensures that the finished product is always of the highest quality
✧ Is willing to sacrifice speed for accuracy
✧ Ensures that any document that leaves her desk will be error free
✧ Refuses to sacrifice quality for volume
✧ Makes a documented record of final outcomes and resolutions
✧ Recommends quality enhancements to customers
✧ Prepares handouts and presentation materials in a meticulous fashion
✧ Receives letters of recommendation from satisfied customers
✧ Detects flaws in raw materials
✧ Remains committed to continuous process improvement
✧ Employs measurement tools that increase efficiency and reduce costs
✧ Consistently "dots the *i*'s and crosses the *t*'s"

Needs Improvement

✧ Tends to get bogged down in "analysis paralysis"
✧ Confuses minor details with the overall purpose of a project

✧ Has been criticized for doing "too thorough a job"
✧ His handwriting is too sloppy to decipher messages accurately
✧ Gets easily side-tracked during routine tasks
✧ Her error rates exceed acceptable thresholds
✧ Fails to take notes of dates and timelines
✧ Misplaces important materials
✧ Fails to obtain approval before making changes in established procedures
✧ Tends to misplace paperwork
✧ Quality of work is below departmental performance standards

Quality Goals

✧ Keep better track of due dates and timelines
✧ Become more consistently aware of quality guidelines
✧ Avoid getting bogged down in minor details
✧ Become more proficient in using technology to increase efficiency
✧ Learn to rely more on documentation than on your memory

Resourcefulness

Meets/Exceeds Expectations

❖ Has developed a network of useful contacts at competitor companies
❖ Knows whom to contact within the company for various needs
❖ Never complains of a lack of resources
❖ Consistently anticipates when and what additional resources may be needed
❖ Takes advantage of shared corporate resources
❖ Achieves economies of scale
❖ Always looks for ways of improving the way we get things done
❖ Has repeatedly introduced cost-saving measures
❖ Takes advantage of free seminars and programs
❖ Allocates resources wisely
❖ Achieves success despite limited organizational resources
❖ Consistently comes in at or under budget
❖ Is able to meet targets without need for additional staff

Needs Improvement

❖ Often underestimates the resources needed for upcoming projects

✧ Has a reputation for hoarding resources
✧ Has trouble remaining within budget
✧ Does not optimize available resources
✧ Resists adjusting his job in light of the department's changing needs
✧ Fails to allocate resources wisely
✧ Makes unreasonable and unjustifiable requests for additional resources
✧ Is reluctant to ask questions when she's not sure of how to do something
✧ Fails to make adequate use of routine office technology

Resourcefulness Goals

✧ Research and identify time-saving resources
✧ Plan for unforeseen expenses and contingencies
✧ Make better use of existing corporate and departmental resources
✧ Use technology to better track performance against budget
✧ Develop alternative solutions for dealing with last-minute changes in plan

Safety

Meets/Exceeds Expectations

- Adheres to all company safety and security policies and regulations
- Remains aware of and reports potential safety hazards
- Complies with all safety recommendations, postings, and requirements
- Consistently provides emergency training to staff
- Duly familiarizes himself with safety instruments and resources
- Disciplines workers who fail to wear appropriate safety gear
- Keeps abreast of industry best practices regarding workplace security
- Minimizes workplace injury and illness occurrences
- Consistently maintains a record of zero safety infractions
- Ensures compliance of staff with company safety programs
- Is familiar with and enforces OSHA regulations
- Prepares cost-benefit analyses of available security systems
- Monitors visitors, suppliers, and vendors to ensure a safe workplace

✧ Reports enterprise-wide safety concerns to local authorities

✧ Leads disaster drills and emergency evacuation planning exercises

✧ Provides safety and security training during new hire orientation

✧ Manages the business continuity planning and disaster recovery programs

✧ Has an excellent personal safety record

✧ His team has a track record of zero safety infractions in the last two years

✧ Regularly publicizes available safety awards and incentives

Needs Improvement

✧ Fails to document potential safety hazards

✧ Does not adhere to environmental safety and health practices

✧ Fails to wear the appropriate safety gear on the shop floor

✧ Often arrives at work without the appropriate safety gear

✧ Has operated machinery without being fully trained to do so

✧ Fails to maintain equipment as per manufacturer's specifications

✧ Fails to keep current on security procedures

✧ Is unable to account for a recent increase in worker injury rates

✧ Is unfamiliar with key statistics for injury types or occurrences

✧ Has failed to take steps to resolve pending hazards in a timely fashion

✧ Does not maintain machinery in compliance with safety manual guidelines

✧ Unnecessarily sacrifices safety for productivity

✧ Fails to strictly enforce environmental regulations

Safety Goals

✧ Recommend effective safety enhancements and corrective actions

✧ Always comply with all safety policies and procedures

✧ Report potential safety hazards immediately

✧ Ensure that your equipment is in proper working order before initiating work

✧ Stringently follow all recommendations outlined in material safety data sheets

✧ Train staff members in hazardous materials (HAZMAT) procedures

✧ Cordon off areas that pose serious safety risks

✧ Request an ergonomic assessment of your work area

✧ Always leave your work area clean and functional at the end of the shift

✧ Communicate any potential malfunctioning equipment at shift change

✧ Maintain your personal tools in proper working order

✧ Regularly respond to inspection queries

✧ Cooperate with safety investigations and audit requests

✧ Follow recommended hygiene practices without exception

✧ Maintain required licenses and certifications in good order

- ❖ Continuously monitor and evaluate environmental and safety data
- ❖ Provide technical and regulatory compliance support
- ❖ Never sacrifice safety for productivity
- ❖ Insist on a "zero tolerance" policy toward safety infractions

Staff Development

Meets/Exceeds Expectations

✧ Readily shares her expertise with staff in order to develop their skills

✧ Makes it safe for staff members to make mistakes and think outside the box

✧ Actively works to identify potential talent gaps in her organization

✧ Remains committed to succession planning

✧ Rotates assignments and uses job shadowing to strengthen staff skills

✧ Encourages staff to develop their professional skills

✧ Ensures that subordinates identify goals and measurable outcomes

✧ Contributes to subordinates' annual development plans

✧ Regularly places support staff in positions of leadership

✧ Demonstrates appreciation of staff contributions and achievements

✧ Allows key subordinates to make presentations on her behalf

✧ Finds ways to publicly recognize individual achievements

✧ Ensures that mistakes become learning opportunities

✧ Creates an environment of trust and camaraderie

- Delegates key responsibilities to subordinates on a rotational basis
- Encourages his direct reports to lead staff meetings
- Allows employees to find new ways of contributing to work
- Promotes the benefits of a diverse workforce
- Encourages cross-training, job shadowing, and rotational assignments

Needs Improvement

- Does not trust his staff to function independently
- Is always too defensive of her people
- Overcompensates for staff weaknesses
- Tends to delegate only mundane and repetitive tasks
- Refuses to accept different points of view from subordinates
- Resists placing subordinates into roles of leadership
- Intimidates and alienates others and squelches individuality
- Fails to create mentoring opportunities for her key performers
- Has not mastered the basics of effective delegation
- Is unsuccessful in developing group camaraderie
- Has been accused of playing favorites with certain subordinates
- Has created an environment where team members cannot motivate themselves

Staff Development Goals

- Provide active feedback and encouragement
- Provide career guidance and coaching to staff

- View delegation as the key to staff development and succession planning
- Recognize each individual's unique contribution to the team
- Ensure that employees continuously develop their breadth and depth of skills
- Carefully monitor what you have delegated
- Delegate what you're good at
- Ensure that your subordinates learn from your key strengths
- Regularly ask employees what new responsibilities they'd like to assume
- Place staff members in position to spearhead key initiatives
- Assume the role of mentor and coach
- Help your staff members prepare for their next move in career progression
- Allow subordinates the opportunity to assume greater responsibilities
- Recognize individual needs and skills when delegating work
- Assign staff to rotational assignments and cross-training
- Foster a greater understanding of others' roles in the organization
- Identify your successor
- Provide more structure, feedback, and direction to your group
- Ensure that subordinates understand their limits and boundaries

Strategic and Critical Thinking Skills

Meets/Exceeds Expectations

✧ Strategically contributes to departmental initiatives

✧ Identifies unique ways of creating value

✧ Realigns work processes in accordance with available resources

✧ Has exceptional reasoning and analysis skills

✧ Thinks through the consequences of recommended courses of action

✧ Thoroughly researches options in terms of risks and consequences

✧ Displays organizational forecasting ability and intuitive insight

✧ Considers both the strategic and tactical aspects of decisions

✧ Always assesses the benefits and consequences of a course of action

✧ Processes information in a disciplined and structured manner

✧ Keeps abreast of competitors' best practices and innovative solutions

✧ Trains others to think long-term

✧ Writes clear and concise proposals for new systems or procedures

✧ Compares departmental performance to industry benchmarks

✧ Measures internal operations using metrics and analytics

✧ Displays both natural inquisitiveness and analytical reasoning skills

✧ Creates accurate forecasts and models

✧ Uses metrics to project budget variances and potential cost overruns

✧ Formulates opinions based on sound mathematical calculations

✧ Strategically partners with management

Needs Improvement

✧ Responds emotionally to critical situations rather than analytically

✧ Avoids any approach or solution that deviates from past practice

✧ Fails to assess issues from a strategic vantage point

✧ Does not approach problem solving in a methodical and logical fashion

✧ Does not consistently avail himself of existing technology

✧ Deals with the symptoms of a problem rather than its underlying causes

✧ Fails to draw sound conclusions

✧ Gives little thought to how decisions might affect other departments

✧ Does not appreciate her own department's capabilities and limitations

✧ Fails to think through the strategic impact of his recommendations

- Does not understand our clients' business drivers and trends
- Is uncomfortable applying proven methodologies in reaching decisions
- Fails to demonstrate sound analytical reasoning abilities

Strategic and Critical Thinking Goals

- Learn to distinguish between strategic and tactical thinking
- Define and communicate the vision for the department
- Develop strategies that reflect our business priorities
- Translate strategies into objectives and action plans
- Gain a deeper understanding of the roles and expectations of our clients
- Strengthen your analytical and critical thinking skills
- Balance strategic with tactical priorities
- Identify significant business trends and patterns
- Learn your customers' businesses inside and out
- Become a subject matter expert
- Routinely request "sneak peeks" into your clients' business challenges
- Keep in sync with your clients' timelines and priorities
- Understand how our company makes and spends money
- Study our annual report to discern activities, trends, and future plans

Supervision

Meets/Exceeds Expectations

✧ Sets clear guidelines and expectations for immediate subordinates

✧ Provides the appropriate amount of structure, direction, and feedback

✧ Confronts problem situations head-on

✧ Uses a direct yet caring approach

✧ Clearly communicates roles and job expectations

✧ Regularly meets one-on-one with staff to show interest in their progress

✧ Outlines action steps and deadlines necessary to reach goals

✧ Commits individual action plans to paper

✧ Regularly measures progress

✧ Ensures that deliverables are achieved

✧ Maintains ongoing and open communication with subordinates

✧ Practices MBWA—Management by Walking Around

✧ Holds regular weekly staff meetings

✧ Readily assumes responsibility for errors

✧ Encourages her staff to use the employee assistance program

- Creates an environment where employees can motivate themselves
- Practices a consensus-building rather than autocratic managerial style

Needs Improvement

- Allows interpersonal conflict among subordinates to fester
- Fails to establish realistic work demands
- Rarely recognizes or appreciates exceptional performance
- Does not proactively address poor staff performance
- Fails to address situations before they become major conflicts
- Works behind closed doors too often
- Is reluctant to provide coaching to direct reports
- Appears inaccessible
- Allows staff members work long hours of unscheduled overtime
- Knows little of what's going on outside his office
- Fails to follow up on subordinates' projects
- Adheres to a "My Way or the Highway" supervisory style

Supervision Goals

- Clearly communicate roles and job expectations
- Set clear and measurable performance goals and objectives
- Inspire employees to take ownership for their performance improvement
- Communicate how individual goals align with organizational objectives

✧ Define "stretch goals" to encourage staff members to think outside the box
✧ Continuously monitor performance
✧ Address problematic performance early on
✧ Encourage open and honest communication
✧ Regularly communicate expectations
✧ Define, direct, and delegate work in a more flexible manner
✧ Effectively prioritize the workload based on current business needs
✧ Regularly give and receive performance feedback
✧ Prioritize the workload with more forethought
✧ Complete annual performance appraisals on a timelier basis
✧ Consistently monitor subordinates' job performance and areas for improvement
✧ Allocate resources more effectively
✧ Be more creative in rewarding and recognizing good work

Teamwork and
Relationship-Building Skills

Meets/Exceeds Expectations

✧ Encourages group cooperation and participation
✧ Builds effective teams
✧ Capitalizes on the talents of team members
✧ Promotes participants into leadership roles
✧ Draws on the strengths of team members
✧ Allows individuals to volunteer in their areas of interest
✧ Treats no suggestion or request as trivial or minor
✧ Shares the glory of success
✧ Treats people with dignity and respect
✧ Successfully builds bridges based on trust and open communication
✧ Provides encouragement when constructive criticism is necessary
✧ Creates strong teams with successful outcomes
✧ Ensures that team members feel united in reaching a common goal
✧ Is very effective in organizing team meetings
✧ Consistently brings out the best in others
✧ Resolves team conflict without drama or histrionics
✧ Attributes achievements to team effort

✧ Insists on mutual respect publicly while resolving problems one-on-one
✧ Encourages open debate and sharing of ideas

Needs Improvement

✧ Clearly prefers to work solo
✧ Attempts to avoid group-related assignments
✧ Is inconsistent in how she allocates tasks to team members
✧ Tends to hog information and resources
✧ Allows team members to get easily sidetracked
✧ Does not encourage or support others who are facing challenges
✧ Fails to interact with the team on a collegial or social basis
✧ Does not readily give credit where credit is due
✧ Tends to "cherry pick" the more appealing assignments
✧ Discourages coworkers from volunteering ideas
✧ Shoots down untested suggestions and recommendations
✧ Demonstrates a domineering work style that puts others off
✧ Has taken credit for other team members' contributions
✧ Becomes antagonistic when her authority is challenged
✧ Engages in public shouting matches when he doesn't get his way
✧ "Talks over" those with conflicting opinions
✧ Has difficulty maintaining confidences

Teamwork and Relationship-Building Goals

✧ Build and lead effective teams
✧ Develop high-performance teams

- Use hands-on coaching and positive reinforcement to create camaraderie
- Regularly monitor team progress
- Provide training to enhance team effectiveness
- Encourage subordinates to assume key leadership roles
- Hold teams accountable for meeting performance goals and objectives
- Take appropriate action to address substandard group performance
- Consistently reward and recognize collective efforts
- Empower teams to embrace and capitalize on change opportunities
- Look for ways to create cross-functional teams to boost productivity
- Foster a sense of shared responsibility
- Set and communicate team vision
- Provide constructive feedback regarding group accountability
- Draw on the strengths of individual contributors
- Strengthen your reputation as a team player
- Develop skills for resolving disruptive conflict among team members

Technical Skills

Meets/Exceeds Expectations

✧ Demonstrates mastery of technical tools and methodologies

✧ Excels at documenting necessary steps and incremental outcomes

✧ Creates results that could be easily replicated

✧ Makes effective use of advanced software tools

✧ Follows the Six Sigma guidelines for controlling business processes

✧ Focuses on increasing efficiency, raising productivity, and reducing costs

✧ Keeps abreast of the latest in office technology

✧ Uses statistical techniques and a methodical approach to solve problems

✧ Adapts well to changes in technology

✧ Actively surfs the Internet for product upgrades and security patches

✧ Effectively analyzes data on a problem-to-solution level

✧ Makes efficient use of technical support

✧ Consistently inputs data with an accuracy rate of 95 percent or better

✧ Provides well-supported reasoning for technical recommendations

- Maintains technical and professional certifications
- Combines advanced technical know-how with solid communication skills

Needs Improvement

- Lacks a sound methodology for diagnosing repetitive problems
- Resists using newly acquired software
- Is slow to switch from paper-based to automated systems
- Fails to apply and practice what he learned in his recent training course
- Has allowed her current license to lapse
- Cannot demonstrate basic mastery of newly installed software
- Resists documenting the steps necessary to repeat a procedure
- Lacks the know-how to diagnose and repair basic systems problems
- Fails to take advantage of training to enhance her technical skills
- Demonstrates only basic technical skills when advanced knowledge is needed
- Is not sufficiently knowledgeable about relevant software tools
- Lacks sufficient technical competence to generate confidence from clients

Technical Skills Goals

- Improve your technical documentation skills
- Keep current on changing technologies and trends

- ✧ Translate technical jargon into user-friendly information
- ✧ Promote new technology as a way to increase efficiency and reduce costs
- ✧ Demonstrate a thorough understanding of the technical aspects of the job
- ✧ Look for creative ways to apply technology to job tasks
- ✧ Complete new system training within the next thirty days
- ✧ Use the online tutorial to master spreadsheet basics
- ✧ Acquire your professional certification within the next year
- ✧ Overcome your resistance to newly introduced technology
- ✧ Automate the paper-based systems currently in use
- ✧ Learn to operate shop machinery more efficiently
- ✧ Train end users so that they can apply new software effectively
- ✧ Retrain in areas where you have become rusty
- ✧ Incorporate the newest technologies into your work

Time Management

Meets/Exceeds Expectations

✧ Consistently approaches his workload in a proactive fashion

✧ Allocates time according to the peaks and valleys of the production cycle

✧ Does not allow distractions or obstacles to get in the way of meeting deadlines

✧ Plans daily activities regularly at 8 am using a daily planner

✧ Ensures that her day is planned as productively as possible

✧ Excels in pushing projects forward despite bureaucratic slowdowns

✧ Syncs PC calendar with personal digital assistant (PDA) to stay on time

✧ Regularly projects specific timetables along with "next steps"

✧ Ensures a consistent workflow despite interruptions

✧ Effectively manages multiple projects rather than one project at a time

✧ Holds his staff accountable for beginning work on time

✧ Sets realistic time frames

✧ Is very reliable at estimating the time necessary to complete tasks

✧ Uses a daily planner to keep herself organized and on time
✧ Delivers product within promised guidelines
✧ Maintains a neat and organized workplace
✧ Handles interruptions well
✧ Effectively allocates time and resources to meet contractual deadlines
✧ Readily maintains key information at his fingertips

Needs Improvement

✧ Gets easily sidetracked and wastes time
✧ Lacks a disciplined approach to time management
✧ Fails to block her day into effective quadrants
✧ Often arrives late and unprepared to staff meetings
✧ Has difficulty accounting for how he spends his time
✧ Asks repetitive questions
✧ Appears overwhelmed at peak time periods
✧ Fails to make use of available technology to automate manual processes
✧ Appears to wander through the workday without much direction or purpose
✧ Is frequently disorganized
✧ Fails to follow meeting schedule start times
✧ Allows meetings to drift
✧ Appears overwhelmed by an average workload
✧ Always appears busy but has little to show for his efforts
✧ Procrastinates whenever a new project must be initiated
✧ Does not pace herself effectively through periods of peak and low activity
✧ Spends too much time away from his desk

Time Management Goals

✧ Take a course on effective time management techniques

✧ Pace yourself to avoid burnout

✧ Demonstrate respect of others' time

✧ Consistently meet or beat deadlines

✧ Manage your time and resources more efficiently

✧ Prioritize tasks according to the degree of current urgency

✧ Weed out and eliminate time wasters

✧ Don't put off to tomorrow what you can do today

✧ Handle higher priority tasks first while maintaining progress on others

✧ Juggle competing priorities more effectively

✧ Keep presentations focused on key agenda items

✧ Take the time to analyze the effectiveness of the meetings you lead

✧ Structure your day into incremental activities

✧ Set aside time to focus on your work without external interruption

✧ Screen callers more thoroughly and qualify the purpose of their calls

✧ Arrive at all staff meetings on time and prepared

PERFORMANCE APPRAISAL PHRASES FOR PARTICULAR TITLES AND ROLES

Accounting and Finance

Accountant

Meets/Exceeds Expectations

✧ Coordinates a high volume of financial data
✧ Excels in a very diverse accounting environment
✧ Answers accounting procedural questions with authority
✧ Interprets the significance behind the numbers
✧ Excels at researching and analyzing financial data
✧ Thoroughly prepares accounting reports and summaries
✧ Completes monthly and quarterly reports on time and error free
✧ Summarizes financial data and tracks trends accurately
✧ Processes a high volume of invoices for payment
✧ Effectively audits his own work
✧ Demonstrates a keen eye for numerical detail
✧ Accurately logs monthly journal entries into the mainframe system
✧ Substantiates financial transactions with clear documentation
✧ Thoroughly reconciles financial discrepancies and variances
✧ Brings significant financial issues to management's immediate attention

❖ Demonstrates broad mastery of appropriate accounting functions
❖ Accurately tracks P&L statements, balance sheets, and other key metrics

Needs Improvement

❖ Fails to maintain accurate financial records and files
❖ Lacks knowledge of generally accepted accounting principles
❖ Shows resistance when asked to customize ad hoc financial reports
❖ Does not consistently follow internal controls
❖ Fails to gain necessary signature approvals for budget variances
❖ Does not consistently complete database backups at appropriate intervals
❖ Fails to research and resolve accounting discrepancies
❖ Fails to approve invoices in a timely manner
❖ Requires ongoing confirmation of repetitive transactional tasks
❖ Exercises little discretion in interpreting financial data
❖ Has failed to maintain confidential financial information
❖ Lacks the necessary software skills to perform at an acceptable level

Auditor

Meets/Exceeds Expectations

✧ Ensures asset protection
✧ Develops and monitors internal control policies and procedures
✧ Documents any shortcomings in the internal financial control system
✧ Skillfully audits internal compliance issues
✧ Thoroughly examines and documents operating practices
✧ Composes audit questionnaires for data security and disaster recovery
✧ Has jumped at the opportunity to receive Sarbanes-Oxley compliance training
✧ Excels at flowcharting business processes and related internal controls
✧ Drives plans for process improvement
✧ Communicates audit findings in a timely manner
✧ Has developed and performed relevant test audits
✧ Readily identifies mitigating and compensating types of controls

Needs Improvement

✧ Fails to consistently perform follow-up audits
✧ Fails to evaluate the status of agreed-upon recommendations
✧ Does not plan and complete audits within established time frames
✧ Lacks the ability to step back from details and see the "big picture"
✧ Does not consistently document and evaluate audit results
✧ Shows a general unwillingness to travel

Bookkeeper

Meets/Exceeds Expectations

✧ Orchestrates a high volume of financial transactions

✧ Accurately performs data entry of overdraft and reconciliation responses

✧ Does an excellent job maintaining the general ledger

✧ Reconciles entries and transfers subsidiary account summaries as needed

✧ Ensures timely processing of payroll

✧ Accurately processes, tracks, and manages payments and commissions

✧ Accesses, prints, and distributes custodian bank statements

✧ Excels in a high-volume accounting environment

✧ Demonstrates proficiency with spreadsheets and accounting software

✧ Accurately prepares reconciliations, internal wire movements, and client reports

✧ Masters diverse bookkeeping functions

✧ Effectively manages all facets of inventory, sales tax, and bank reconciliation

Needs Improvement

✧ Has not demonstrated sufficient expertise with financial software

✧ Tends to neglect the mail sorting and distribution part of her job

✧ Has difficulty balancing A/P, A/R, payroll, and cash management duties

✧ Often falls behind in general ledger analysis and financial statement preparation
✧ Does not demonstrate a solid understanding of bookkeeping principles
✧ Fails to display acceptable customer service when interacting with creditors

Controller

Meets/Exceeds Expectations

- Maximizes return on financial assets
- Approves budgets and initiates corrective action as required
- Directs the preparation of financial data
- Effectively evaluates internal controls
- Ensures compliance with company guidelines
- Regularly compares actual results to forecasts
- Readily accounts for variances
- Regularly prepares financial schedules for inclusion in supplemental reports
- Supplies accurate information for use in income projections
- Ensures that computer systems are in sync with the general ledger
- Effectively tracks amortization costs versus expected lifetime revenues
- Coordinates communication between financial reporting and operational finance
- Reviews the assumptions and computations used for the scenario reserve

Needs Improvement

- Fails to check calculations for overall reasonableness
- Fails to interpret financial data accurately
- Does not initiate corrective actions on a timely basis
- Does not consistently achieve budget objectives

- ✧ Is slow to advise management on needed actions
- ✧ Has fallen behind in his understanding of new legislation
- ✧ Puts forward overly optimistic income projections
- ✧ Has not yet established appropriate disclosure controls and procedures
- ✧ Has failed to share significant data with corporate auditors

Credit and Collections Manager

Meets/Exceeds Expectations

- Duly protects our organization's assets
- Attentively reviews and supervises collection activities
- Verifies the financial status of credit applicants
- Actively approves credit
- Skillfully negotiates payment plans with delinquent accounts
- Collects all accounts receivable open items to improve cash flow
- Regularly processes waivers and lien releases
- Recommends approval or rejection of credit
- Readily reviews credit applications for prospective customers
- Establishes credit limits in accordance with company policies
- Accurately maintains credit history, bankruptcy, and bad debt write-off files
- Promptly researches credit histories of existing and potential customers
- Effectively persuades customers to pay amounts due on credit accounts
- Duly notifies customers of delinquent accounts
- Solicits payment or negotiates extensions of credit, as necessary

Needs Improvement

- Is slow to post payments to customers' accounts
- Does not accurately communicate credit limits and credit problems

- ✧ Fails to document improved cash flow metrics and billing refinements
- ✧ Does not process the placement of credit holds or requirements for prepayments
- ✧ Fails to block order placements from customers with credit problems

Financial Analyst

Meets/Exceeds Expectations

✧ Effectively forecasts business trends

✧ Coordinates all aspects of budgeting, financial valuations, and reporting

✧ Collects and monitors competitive performance data against forecasts

✧ Assists in business planning and acquisitions modeling

✧ Identifies opportunities for product expansion

✧ Skillfully prepares division's fiscal year budget

✧ Effectively analyzes past operating budgets and variances

✧ Projects future expenditures accurately

✧ Aggressively monitors and adjusts departmental expenditures

✧ Develops future cost-control guidelines

✧ Develops computer applications to maximize user convenience

✧ Addresses accounting irregularities and potential conflicts of interest

✧ Assesses the potential financial impact of contractual obligations

Needs Improvement

✧ Has difficulty presenting detailed financial information in layman's terms

✧ Fails to summarize economic information and trends

✧ Misses opportunities to monitor overhead expenses through effective cost analysis
✧ Fails to identify and account for budget variances
✧ Shies away from internal-audit and sales-planning areas of responsibility

Human Resources

➤ ◄

Benefits Administrator

Meets/Exceeds Expectations

✧ Successfully administers all aspects of our company's
  benefits program
✧ Deals well with a sometimes aggressive and overly demanding workforce
✧ Proactively studies industry trends and developments in
  benefits
✧ Secures the greatest return on investment for our benefit
  dollars
✧ Ensures that employees fully understand their benefits
  options
✧ Promotes the benefits of participating in the company's
  401(k) program
✧ Publicizes and draws attention to some of the lesser-
  known benefits programs
✧ Ensures that we get maximum value for the benefits that
  we offer
✧ Calculates future costs based on cost of living and benefits
  acceleration rates
✧ Closely monitors changing legal requirements and new
  legislation

- Networks regularly with benefits consulting services
- Stays abreast of trends and best practices in benefits design
- Seeks qualified outside counsel when needed to advise management
- Maintains accurate benefit records and usage rates
- Fully complies with HIPAA requirements
- Ensures that benefit programs comply with statutory requirements
- Reconciles benefit statement variances
- Summarizes complex data and makes sound recommendations

Needs Improvement

- Does not consistently interpret benefit policies accurately
- Often fails to recognize the precedent-setting nature of her decisions
- Tends to delegate more complex calculations to his subordinates
- Falls behind in reviewing and approving billing statements
- May allow a benefit proposal to languish rather than pushing it through
- Does not aggressively explore new benefit options and alternatives
- Has failed to ensure that our insurance carrier raise its level of customer service
- Does not respond promptly to employee questions and concerns

Compensation Analyst

Meets/Exceeds Expectations

- Maintains the integrity of the corporate pay structure
- Ensures that all internal compensation decisions are justifiable and fair
- Accurately calculates pay grades and ranges
- Regularly participates in third-party compensation surveys
- Thoroughly documents external market as well as internal equity salary data
- Verifies that operating and capital budgets can support recommended courses of action
- Excels in the areas of base pay data analysis
- Regularly surveys comparative compensation practices at competitor companies
- Explains to supervisors the necessary considerations in awarding promotions
- Successfully enforces merit raise and incentive guidelines
- Regularly ensures that job descriptions are up to date
- Confirms that job requirements for open positions are valid
- Compares proposed pay increases with budget and flags potential variances
- Ensures that all compensation-related decisions receive appropriate corporate approval

Needs Improvement

- Cannot always account for variances in compensation rates

✧ Has difficulty recommending proposals for equity adjustments

✧ Fails to demonstrate full comprehension of our sales incentive plan

✧ Resists considering potential exceptions to the pay grade structure

✧ Has inappropriately shared compensation data with other supervisors

✧ Does not keep up to date on trends in compensation management

✧ Relies on surveys rather than on data from active market comparisons

Employee and Labor Relations Representative

Meets/Exceeds Expectations

- ✧ Strategically partners with department managers to reduce staff turnover
- ✧ "Manages out" substandard performers via progressive disciplinary actions
- ✧ Performs pre- and post-layoff analyses during periods of reductions in force
- ✧ Works well with outside counsel to vet layoff proposals
- ✧ Investigates and evaluates employee complaints in an objective fashion
- ✧ Successfully conducts training workshops for first-time supervisors
- ✧ Makes written records of employee and supervisor statements and actions
- ✧ Provides advice and guidance that is consistent with policies and past practices
- ✧ Successfully brokers disputes between supervisors and staff members
- ✧ Creates a safe and neutral zone for employees with complaints or concerns
- ✧ Maintains an environment of trust and open communication
- ✧ Treats employees who have problems with dignity and respect
- ✧ Skillfully manages workers' expectations
- ✧ Generates few if any union grievances or unfair labor practice charges
- ✧ Effectively managed the preparation of the new employee handbook

❖ Reduced the number of active grievances by 40 percent in eighteen months

❖ Successfully encourages greater cooperation between union and management

Needs Improvement

❖ Continues to have difficulty administering leaves of absence

❖ Confuses workers' compensation, FMLA, and ADA guidelines

❖ Has breached confidentiality, exacerbating the problem and lessening trust

❖ Does not return phone calls to internal clients in a timely manner

❖ Lacks the necessary knowledge of federal and state employment laws

❖ Fails to provide appropriate advice and counsel

❖ Has not gained the trust and confidence of internal clients

❖ Acts as an extension of management rather than an employee advocate

❖ Fails to keep records of the resolution of conflicts and complaints

Recruiter (Corporate)

Meets/Exceeds Expectations

- Spearheads strategic workforce planning efforts
- Attracts a broad range of qualified applicants
- Scouts exceptional talent
- Effectively monitors staffing projections, turnover trends, and talent gaps
- Identifies succession planning needs
- Ensures that published job requirements are up to date and accurate
- Regularly posts company job openings
- Attends diversity job fairs and conducts college campus recruitment
- Coordinates exploratory interviews for exceptional candidates
- Effectively screens and interviews selected candidates
- Administers tests to determine technical suitability
- Strives to match a candidate's personality to a department's culture
- Reduces costs by assessing and adjusting her recruitment outreach efforts
- Measures staffing effectiveness using cost-per-hire and turnover metrics
- Finds creative ways to encourage prior employers to provide references
- Immediately notifies management of problems with background checks
- Successfully negotiates salary offers

- Accurately retains applicant flow results and EEO statistics
- Follows up regularly with new recruits throughout the introductory period
- Complies with all federal, state, and local employment laws
- Provides training on the do's and don'ts of interviewing and selection
- Successfully matches internal talent with current job openings

Needs Improvement

- Fails to pre-qualify candidates' salary expectations
- Often loses candidates to counteroffers after the completion of a search
- Refers unqualified applicants to hiring managers
- Fails to gather sufficient initial hiring data from hiring managers
- Fails to provide agencies with adequate information to successfully screen applicants
- Falls short of diversity outreach targets for female and minority recruitment
- Regularly falls behind in paying advertising and temp agency bills
- Fails to elicit sufficient information in candidate interviews
- Is not sufficiently aware of employment laws
- Often fails to "sell" the company to desirable job candidates

Training and Organizational Development Specialist

Meets/Exceeds Expectations

✧ Excels at identifying training and development needs

✧ Partners with department managers to understand their unique challenges

✧ Successfully performs needs analysis, program design, and implementation

✧ Analyzes weekly production ratios and quarterly per desk averages

✧ Successfully forecasts strategic workforce planning needs

✧ Has built a training program from scratch based on survey feedback

✧ Maintains a network of industry trainers and executive coaches

✧ Stays abreast of the latest training programs and tools

✧ Exhibits outstanding platform skills

✧ Delivers training materials in an effective and enjoyable format

✧ Ensures that newly learned skills are consistently applied

✧ Delivers state-of-the-art training methodologies and techniques

✧ Successfully leads our department's "train the trainer" efforts

✧ Demonstrates a "best practices" approach in each learning module

✧ Suggests new alignments for existing departments and work groups

✧ Creates awareness of the importance of succession planning

❖ Encouraged our CEO to adopt an "open book" approach to management
❖ Routinely evaluates the impact of training on business results

Needs Improvement

❖ Fails to identify opportunities for work restructuring or job redesign
❖ Fails to identify opportunities for team building and management training
❖ Has not been able to improve excessive turnover and absenteeism rates
❖ Does not consistently evaluate training effectiveness
❖ Fails to follow up with trainees to ensure practical concept application
❖ Does not maintain training equipment and physical facilities
❖ Has not received acceptable evaluation scores
❖ Fails to adopt new training methodologies
❖ Resists using survey feedback data when developing new training material

Information Technology

➤ ◄

Data Entry Operator

Meets/Exceeds Expectations

✧ Excels at alphanumeric data entry
✧ Prepares source data for computer entry in a timely and accurate manner
✧ Enters customer and account data with a minimum of errors
✧ Obtains accurate data from sales orders, invoices, and licenses
✧ Conducts mass updates of current database records with minimal errors
✧ Accurately generates mass mailing lists
✧ Skillfully creates and populates database fields
✧ Regularly prepares and sorts source documents
✧ Readily contacts preparers of source documents to resolve discrepancies
✧ Diligently keeps track of source documents
✧ Regularly reviews error reports and enters corrections into the computer
✧ Carefully compiles, sorts, and verifies accuracy of data to be entered

Needs Improvement

- ❖ Rarely purges files to eliminate duplication of data
- ❖ Does not consistently file or route source documents after entry
- ❖ Often fails to compare data entered with source documents
- ❖ Tends to miss detecting errors due to carelessness
- ❖ Reenters an excessive amount of data due to initial entry inaccuracies
- ❖ Needs to be reminded to secure information by completing database backups

Database Administrator

Meets/Exceeds Expectations

✧ Regularly monitors multiple database servers and troubleshoots errors

✧ Skillfully performs quality reviews of database changes

✧ Coordinates backup and recovery as well as disaster planning initiatives

✧ Regularly implements physical database changes

✧ Configures and installs software and administration tools

✧ Oversees database schema impacts, application impacts, and data storage

✧ Provides configuration support for new applications and database structures

✧ Regularly monitors distributed databases for performance

✧ Effectively manages all aspects of our site, including design and applications

✧ Successfully serves as performance analyst and database architect

✧ Understands database applications and operating system interactions

✧ Troubleshoots problems in clustered application service environments

Needs Improvement

✧ Appears to be less skilled at query optimization and schema design

✧ Does not proactively monitor database performance and maintenance

- ❖ Has difficulty functioning in a high-volume production service environment
- ❖ Lacks proficiency in shell scripting and programming
- ❖ Requires ongoing support as a capacity planner and as a monitoring tools developer
- ❖ Has difficulty handling out-of-band requests
- ❖ Avoids making herself available for periodic on-call duty

Help Desk Coordinator

Meets/Exceeds Expectations

✧ Handles all inquiries on software, hardware, and network operations

✧ Accurately responds to users and diagnoses problems

✧ Methodically performs problem research, recognition, and resolution steps

✧ Accurately opens tickets, triages, and escalates work requests

✧ Consistently follows procedural guidelines

✧ Logically determines initial assignment status

✧ Readily assigns open service ticket requests

✧ Accurately logs calls, diagnoses problems, and provides timely feedback

✧ Clearly communicates technical information to nontechnical clients

✧ Participates in new product beta and delta testing and documentation

✧ Handily resolves complex problems

Needs Improvement

✧ Often fails to assign more complex problems to second-level support

✧ Has difficulty recognizing requests that fall outside his area of responsibility

✧ Fails to follow up with clients about the status of open service ticket requests

✧ Has yet to demonstrate a thorough understanding of help-desk operations

- ❖ Lacks knowledge of requisite help-desk tools, processes, and methodologies
- ❖ Does not exhibit creativity and flexibility in problem solving

Programmer Analyst

Meets/Exceeds Expectations

✧ Successfully designs and tests technical solutions to business problems

✧ Skillfully integrates processes and systems into existing applications

✧ Demonstrates advanced analytical and problem-solving skills

✧ Resolves issues only after assessing possible systems impact

✧ Provides technical guidance and support to junior developers

✧ Ensures that all standards are met for a variety of complex applications

✧ Ensures high quality programs

✧ Designs, codes, tests, debugs, documents, and maintains programs

✧ Prepares detailed software specifications

✧ Troubleshoots incidents reported by end users

✧ Effectively communicates project status with clients and peers

✧ Provides full life-cycle support to new processes and systems

Needs Improvement

✧ Fails to grasp highly complex systems

✧ Has difficulty processing technical solutions to meet business requirements

✧ Lacks solid relational database skills
✧ Will not adjust his schedule to accommodate off-hour systems
✧ Has difficulty modifying moderately complex information systems
✧ Has not achieved unit testing of developed code by the stated deadline
✧ Has not consistently documented and tracked the status of open assignments

Project Manager

Meets/Exceeds Expectations

❖ Successfully plans and coordinates teams for multiple IT projects

❖ Efficiently manages time lines and budgets

❖ Analyzes, designs, and implements cost-effective solutions

❖ Thoroughly conducts systems analysis

❖ Facilitates resolution of internal control problems

❖ Serves as a liaison between vendors and internal personnel

❖ Excels at creating and managing project plans

❖ Strategically deploys and manages enterprise-wide management platforms

❖ Provides direction for development, migration, and integration activities

❖ Facilitates communication between program office and service territories

❖ Regularly develops and fosters business partnerships with internal customers

❖ Establishes accurate and well-communicated implementation procedures

❖ Sees projects through from inception to deployment

❖ Serves as the primary IT driver for delivering enhancements and new functionality

Needs Improvement

❖ Fails to keep management abreast of schedule and budget challenges

- ❖ Has not met expectations in technical presentations and proposal writing
- ❖ Does not consistently define clients' requirements
- ❖ Fails to keep the internal Software/QA team engaged in clients' goals
- ❖ Does not stay abreast of new trends in technology

Systems Analyst

Meets/Exceeds Expectations

❖ Successfully analyzes and defines application programs
❖ Skillfully designs data processing procedures
❖ Effectively writes and reviews programming specifications
❖ Accurately codes new and existing computer programs
❖ Determines system specifications
❖ Recommends equipment changes
❖ Prepares system flow charts
❖ Successfully analyzes complex problems and defines application programs
❖ Masters all phases of the project development life cycle
❖ Readily supports the development, testing, and implementation of new systems
❖ Recommends enhancements to existing systems
❖ Meets implementation dates and deliverables as planned and under budget
❖ Regularly meets with users to gather requirements for project definitions
❖ Carefully analyzes existing procedures before making appropriate recommendations
❖ Consistently abides by change control requirements for application development

Needs Improvement

❖ Lacks sufficient knowledge of project management protocols

✧ Fails to define new databases or modify existing applications, as required

✧ Is ineffective as liaison between database users and developers

✧ Has difficulty refining data and converting it into a programmable form

✧ Is reluctant to provide general IT support on an ongoing basis

Legal

➡ ⬅

Attorney

Meets/Exceeds Expectations

✧ Provides prompt and reliable legal advice and counsel
✧ Skillfully drafts and reviews legal agreements to secure corporate interests
✧ Regularly analyzes legal claims made against the company
✧ Works effectively with outside counsel
✧ Anticipates legal risks of pending business deals
✧ Masters even the most complex litigation
✧ Successfully resolves pending issues and ties up loose ends
✧ Serves as a rich source of institutional knowledge in terms of past practices
✧ Develops a high volume of new clients through a network of business contacts
✧ Reviews, interprets, and analyzes agreements with a keen eye for detail
✧ Skillfully negotiates and drafts contract modifications
✧ Responds to subpoenas in a consistent and timely fashion
✧ Is effective in the courtroom and articulate in instructing a jury about the law

Needs Improvement

- Does not respond to legal queries in a timely manner
- Fails to secure the company's interests
- Fails to ensure budget compliance with contractual requirements
- Does not alert management to potential legal risks and litigation
- Cannot yet orchestrate outside counsel in large-scale projects
- Resists working the expected number of hours for a first-year attorney
- Appears condescending when dealing with nonlawyers in other departments
- Fails to consider past agreements when recommending courses of action

Contract Analyst

Meets/Exceeds Expectations

✧ Skillfully administers and maintains the contract management system
✧ Flags urgent contractual items for immediate review
✧ Consistently tracks and logs all pertinent case information
✧ Inputs newly acquired data into the departmental tracking system
✧ Accurately drafts modification memos
✧ Consistently refers any problems encountered to senior management
✧ Carefully evaluates revision agreements
✧ Incorporates proposed amendments into contract revisions
✧ Interprets redline agreements accurately and precisely
✧ Consistently tracks and saves all previous versions of documents
✧ Regularly drafts pro forma documents for my signature
✧ Skillfully analyzes incoming agreements for inconsistencies

Needs Improvement

✧ Does not thoroughly analyze contracts to identify potential problems
✧ Regularly falls behind in updating contract files
✧ Misplaces incoming change orders, interim agreements, and amendments

- ✧ Continues to struggle with legal terminology
- ✧ Fails to identify discrepancies that fall outside of contract guidelines
- ✧ Interprets revision agreements haphazardly

Legal Secretary

Meets/Exceeds Expectations

- Provides legal secretarial support consistently and responsibly
- Handles all matters relating to the preparation of correspondence
- Revises contracts accurately
- Tracks document modifications, including footnotes and cross-references
- Demonstrates exceptionally strong word processing skills
- Effectively prioritizes my schedule
- Actively screens outside phone calls
- Clearly sets clients' expectations in terms of my ability to respond to their needs
- Demonstrates outstanding organizational skills
- Creates high quality visuals for bound and indexed client presentations
- Accurately processes expense reports and travel authorizations
- Willingly assists with billable hour computations
- Effectively manipulates pro forma templates
- Demonstrates a keen interest in business and legal affairs

Needs Improvement

- Has difficulty taking shorthand or using the Dictaphone
- Becomes confused when interpreting redline documents

- Has difficulty reading his own writing and tracking his own changes
- Can be too abrupt with clients and outside callers
- Tends to pick and choose the attorneys for whom she wants to work

Paralegal

Meets/Exceeds Expectations

- Excels at providing litigation support
- Exercises sound judgment in preparing agendas for weekly legal meetings
- Drafts interrogatories, schedules depositions, and prepares document indices
- Regularly evaluates and responds to requests from outside parties
- Successfully manages a high volume of cases
- Serves as a helpful communication link with outside counsel
- Has a thorough understanding of the steps involved in civil litigation
- Successfully assists with litigation, administrative, and compliance matters
- Regularly prepares affidavits of documents and maintains document files
- Processes bills and vouchers from outside counsel and related vendors
- Assists with discovery, including the review and production of documents
- Monitors court dockets
- Prepares and files proofs of claim, pleadings, and fee applications
- Prepares and maintains corporate records

Needs Improvement

- Lacks focus when reading and interpreting contracts
- Fails to provide the departmental legal assistant with clear instructions

- ✧ Fails to monitor licensees to ensure that they fulfill their contractual obligations
- ✧ Has not taken the time to bring her contract files up to date
- ✧ Fails to extract applicable information when reading and interpreting contracts
- ✧ Does not demonstrate sufficient flexibility to handle clerical duties

Manufacturing

➤ ◂

Assembly and Packaging Technician

Meets/Exceeds Expectations

✧ Accurately receives, scans, and inspects product
✧ Assembles approximately 500 parts per hour with minimum error
✧ Re-scans and repackages products according to company guidelines
✧ Satisfactorily performs limited mechanical assembly
✧ Handles small parts very carefully and accounts for all components
✧ Demonstrates appropriate knowledge and skill with power and hand tools
✧ Reads blueprints and schematics
✧ Readily troubleshoots, repairs, and rebuilds units
✧ Rotates job duties in the areas of assembly, inspection, and auditing
✧ Recommends and implements changes to the assembly processes
✧ Works with manufacturing engineers to convert metric to US standards
✧ Identifies requirements for special tools, fixtures, and gauges

✧ Provides shop floor supervision as the shop grows
✧ Fixes machines when they break down
✧ Loads and unloads trucks when asked

Needs Improvement

✧ Is reluctant to assist in the areas of machine operation and packaging
✧ Fails to consistently inspect products before they leave the warehouse
✧ Is unable to solve a variety of machining and assembly problems
✧ Lacks sufficient knowledge of assembly processes and equipment
✧ Appears dissatisfied with the repetitive nature of his work

Distribution Manager

Meets/Exceeds Expectations

- ❖ Plans and directs all warehouse operations
- ❖ Ensures that job responsibilities are promptly and efficiently carried out
- ❖ Oversees the proper inventory control of all warehoused products
- ❖ Ensures that warehouse operations comply with federal, state, and local law
- ❖ Maintains accurate physical inventories of all company products
- ❖ Consistently meets diverse shipment demands
- ❖ Ensures that all pending orders are scheduled within 24 hours
- ❖ Delivers orders within seven days of receipt
- ❖ Oversees product master scheduling and global distribution of products
- ❖ Makes management aware of material and labor shortages
- ❖ Provides input for revenue estimates and demand projections
- ❖ Successfully achieves 24/7 coverage to assure timely shipments to customers
- ❖ Responsibly oversees warehousing inventory control and fulfillment
- ❖ Ensures that housekeeping meets company and FDA standards

Needs Improvement

- ❖ Fails to retain accurate paperwork for inventory receipt and pick-ups

✧ Has difficulty calculating discounts, interest, commissions, and percentages
✧ Is disadvantaged by a lack of supply chain management and APICS certification
✧ Fails to consistently meet goals for on-time shipment
✧ Does not promptly report rescheduling needs caused by backlogs

MANUFACTURING

Equipment Technician

Meets/Exceeds Expectations

 ✧ Prioritizes and completes needed repairs
 ✧ Makes repairs in accordance with operating manuals
 ✧ Identifies local parts distributors and service vendors
 ✧ Purchases supplies within approved dollar authority
 ✧ Maintains sufficient inventory of readily used supplies
 ✧ Regularly advises management of needed equipment purchase and repair
 ✧ Performs warranty work in accordance with manufacturers' specifications
 ✧ Attends training and safety programs offered by equipment manufacturers
 ✧ Educates personnel on proper maintenance and use of equipment
 ✧ Ensures that completed work meets blueprint and schematic specifications
 ✧ Provides technical support on factory-assembly production equipment
 ✧ Routinely implements preventive maintenance procedures
 ✧ Identifies and resolves equipment failures
 ✧ Supports field engineering with equipment and process enhancements

Needs Improvement

 ✧ Fails to adequately anticipate and diagnose equipment problems

- ✧ Does not consistently obtain and retain warranty certifications
- ✧ Lacks the appropriate safety orientation for hand and power tools
- ✧ Repeatedly fails to sanitize rental equipment upon return
- ✧ Often avoids assisting in loading and receiving inventory

Machinist

Meets/Exceeds Expectations

✧ Initiates procedures for machine setup and operation sequences

✧ Accurately selects, measures, assembles, and sets up cutting tools

✧ Efficiently mounts, aligns, and secures fixtures and materials

✧ Loads programs into machine control in order to start automatic operation

✧ Regulates cutting depth, speeds, and coolant flow during machining operations

✧ Confers with programmer to resolve machining or programming problems

✧ Has detailed knowledge of precision measuring instruments

✧ Inspects critical dimensions on work pieces as prescribed by setup data

✧ Provides support in the areas of assembly, sourcing, and errands

✧ Skillfully operates numerically controlled machine tools

✧ Performs progressive machine operations to exacting tolerances

✧ Works well from drawings and specifications

✧ Regularly records and documents required information in production sheets

Needs Improvement

✧ Is reluctant to participate in on-the-job training provided by team leaders

- Fails to maintain a clean work area
- Does not regularly observe all safety rules and company regulations
- Lacks the necessary technical training in the machine tool trades
- Does not demonstrate sufficient skills in shop math and blueprint reading

Manufacturing Supervisor

Meets/Exceeds Expectations

✧ Regularly ensures that production goals are met
✧ Maintains safety, quality, and productivity goals
✧ Prioritizes production schedules
✧ Oversees product introduction, equipment efficiency, and materials supply
✧ Keeps engineering informed of product difficulties or quality problems
✧ Ensures that master batch formulas are executed and documented correctly
✧ Promotes safety awareness
✧ Reviews processes with the intent of improving quality, economy, and efficiency
✧ Regularly ensures that quality assurance standards are maintained
✧ Analyzes continuous process improvement controls
✧ Routinely performs quality checks
✧ Communicates problems during shift change meetings
✧ Plans and schedules manpower to meet production demands
✧ Ensures that expenses do not exceed budgeted amounts

Needs Improvement

✧ Fails to confirm that master batch formulas are accurate
✧ Neglects performing investigations and root cause analysis

✧ Does not regularly ensure that subordinates are trained on jobs assigned

✧ Does not maintain a clean working environment

✧ Fails to enforce strict adherence to all safety practices

✧ Does not demonstrate adequate control over departmental costs

Master Scheduler

Meets/Exceeds Expectations

- Regularly maintains planning and master production schedules
- Ensures that specified production and inventory levels are achieved
- Successfully schedules facility workload to help meet service goals
- Helps gain management approval for new master scheduling policies
- Conducts regular master schedule meetings
- Accurately produces processing plans
- Calculates facility capacity, materials availability, and due dates
- Proactively investigates future department level scheduling
- Synchronizes master schedule, floor schedule, and shipping schedule
- Coordinates materials, tooling, and equipment resources for upcoming jobs
- Compiles and summarizes production and downtime data
- Highlights problems with production reporting and suggests solutions
- Expedites material shortages to meet customer delivery requirements
- Coordinates production planning in light of backlog and forecast requirements

Needs Improvement

✧   Fails to initiate corrective scheduling actions

✧   Does not readily volunteer input into the strategic production plan

✧   Lacks sufficient understanding of plant flexibility requirements

✧   Fails to routinely confirm delivery dates for new or changed orders

✧   Does not maintain the shop schedule at order level

Production Control Assistant

Meets/Exceeds Expectations

✧ Regularly prints and batches production orders
✧ Ensures that part numbers meet spec requirements
✧ Enters part numbers into the system in a timely fashion
✧ Collects and sorts production records
✧ Compiles appropriate production control reports
✧ Accurately calculates and reports daily production numbers
✧ Assists in creating and maintaining procedures to ease daily operation
✧ Diligently maintains data integrity of item master
✧ Acts as a liaison between inventory control and internal customer groups
✧ Coordinates and communicates order cancellations
✧ Facilitates order queries and releases
✧ Efficiently dispatches approved rush requests
✧ Accurately calculates scrap, waste, and defect data
✧ Regularly researches historical data

Needs Improvement

✧ Fails to organize receipts of vendor invoices
✧ Does not consistently process freight damage/loss reports
✧ Fails to assist with backorder notifications and log entries
✧ Does not regularly secure information by completing database back-ups
✧ Is often delinquent in managing daily exception reports

Production Lead

Meets/Exceeds Expectations

✧ Regularly oversees shift activities
✧ Ensures the safe operation of production lines and machinery
✧ Meets production goals, quality, and cost objectives
✧ Regularly ensures that line personnel are thoroughly trained
✧ Manages the daily assignment of nonexempt manufacturing personnel
✧ Organizes line workload and staffing depending on product priority
✧ Ensures that quality standards in materials and fabrication methods are maintained
✧ Handles all aspects of start-up, operation, and preventive maintenance
✧ Assists in the development and refinement of manufacturing processes
✧ Diligently tracks production efforts
✧ Maintains compliance with established ISO procedures
✧ Ensures that assignments are performed within established safety guidelines
✧ Minimizes excess material on the floor
✧ Coordinates and monitors the availability of operation supplies and equipment

Needs Improvement

✧ Fails to verify that only authorized documentation is available on the line

✧ Does not regularly inform employees of deviations or changes

✧ Does not notify management regarding employee concerns or recommendations

✧ Fails to ensure that personnel are properly trained

✧ Has difficulty keeping assigned areas clean and organized

✧ Fails to handle minor repairs

Production Supervisor

Meets/Exceeds Expectations

✧ Achieves plant goals for safety, quality, and productivity
✧ Utilizes key operating indicators for control of product cost
✧ Manages material usage, machine downtime, and expenditure control
✧ Successfully oversees production scheduling
✧ Improves materials tracking
✧ Regularly establishes work schedules
✧ Manages all production activities to ensure excellent results
✧ Ensures that quality assurance specifications are met
✧ Supervises hourly affiliated employees according to union contract guidelines
✧ Aggressively investigates labor, cost, and process variances
✧ Oversees packaging, shipping, facility maintenance, and environmental monitoring
✧ Trains operators to maintain safety protocols
✧ Effectively communicates the proper procedures and steps in building product

Needs Improvement

✧ Fails to produce quality product
✧ Lacks a functional knowledge of lean manufacturing concepts
✧ Neglects to keep the night shift informed of production progressions
✧ Fails to build products to company specifications
✧ Gets overwhelmed by the overlapping demands of production and scheduling

R&D Engineer

Meets/Exceeds Expectations

- Develops new concepts from initial design to market release
- Regularly conducts feasibility studies
- Skillfully writes and submits intellectual property patents
- Maintains detailed documentation throughout all phases of research and development (R&D)
- Investigates and evaluates existing technologies
- Thoroughly researches, develops, and designs materials and components
- Reviews and coordinates vendor activities to support development
- Strives to improve the quality and performance of existing products
- Readily assists in the development of new products
- Develops conceptual and detailed designs
- Regularly conducts test programs to evaluate product performance
- Develops accurate and cost-effective diagrams and layout drawings
- Ensures that engineering specifications conform to customer requirements
- Envisions and develops tests to acquire functional data on new designs
- Drafts prototype machined parts and tooling

Needs Improvement

- Has difficulty converting raw data into refined data
- Fails to demonstrate sufficient knowledge of tooling and instrumentation

- ❖ Lacks an understanding of data acquisition methods
- ❖ Has difficulty integrating concepts into final products
- ❖ Fails to execute project deliverables on a timely basis

Supply Chain Manager

Meets/Exceeds Expectations

- Effectively plans and directs all aspects of supply chain initiatives
- Retains complete responsibility over the supply chain process
- Skillfully evaluates advanced planning and scheduling procedures
- Oversees storage capabilities, scheduling, warehousing, and shipping
- Plans and schedules manufacturing capacity
- Ensures that company purchases are maximized
- Effectively manages supplier relationships
- Is proficient in using e-commerce/information technology
- Drives continuous improvement initiatives within the local supply chain group
- Establishes goals that are in line with lean and demand flow methodologies
- Successfully coordinates activities with plant manufacturing
- Consistently ensures on-time completion of allocated master production plans

Needs Improvement

- Lacks experience in a consumer-oriented make-to-stock environment
- Fails to thoroughly involve himself in all facets of the commodity life cycle

✧ Does not formulate adequate plant production plans
✧ Has not fully participated in driving supply chain automation
✧ Fails to regularly practice safety-conscious behaviors

Technical Writer

Meets/Exceeds Expectations

- Accurately researches, outlines, and writes technical documents
- Regularly develops, produces, and maintains reference manuals
- Develops style guides and service guides
- Provides thorough technical instruction with users' manuals
- Skillfully develops drawings, sketches, diagrams, and charts
- Oversees product installation, maintenance, and repair
- Uses consistent writing style and accurate grammar, spelling, and punctuation
- Drafts documents that conform to established master templates
- Ensures that all documentation is accurate and complete
- Performs thorough research when initiating an assigned project
- Determines needed scope, content, purpose, and audience
- Uses functional specifications and source materials to design key concepts
- Regularly works with the printer to review and approve document proofs

Needs Improvement

- Lacks familiarity with industry-standard desktop publishing tools

- ❖ Fails to use appropriate resource materials during the writing process
- ❖ Is unable to develop end-user documents from start to finish
- ❖ Does not complete final documentation on schedule
- ❖ Fails to maintain version control of documents

Operations

➤ ◄

Administrative Assistant

Meets/Exceeds Expectations

✧ Does a very thorough job administering office services
✧ Effectively maintains the work flow in our department
✧ Quickly resolves administrative problems
✧ Provides consistent customer service support
✧ Ensures that all clients are treated with the utmost respect and professionalism
✧ Thoroughly plans, organizes, and schedules our department's workload
✧ Flags hot issues that require management's immediate attention
✧ Proofreads and edits documents and makes necessary corrections
✧ Always makes visitors feel comfortable
✧ Maintains an up-to-date and organized filing system
✧ Excels at coordinating a high volume of meetings
✧ Keeps me informed of updates and last-minute changes in schedule
✧ Highlights pertinent articles in trade journals and on the Internet

✧ Consistently monitors office inventories and anticipates needed supplies

Needs Improvement

✧ Falls behind in processing expense reports
✧ Fails to screen calls effectively
✧ Misspells callers' names and transposes telephone numbers
✧ Has a very difficult time prioritizing the workload
✧ Maintains a disorganized desk
✧ Has difficulty locating necessary documents on short notice
✧ Causes unnecessary delays by having to do things twice
✧ Requires a concrete outline of specific instructions
✧ Fails to keep me informed of schedule changes
✧ Mislabels files and misses typos in correspondence and reports
✧ Pays too little attention to details
✧ Has not tried to advance her technical knowledge and skills

Customer Service Representative

Meets/Exceeds Expectations

- Excels at serving customers
- Provides product and service information in a timely fashion
- Readily resolves product and service discrepancies
- Enhances customers' sales and purchasing satisfaction
- Consistently recommends ways to improve customer service
- Creates a welcome and open dialogue with prospects
- Questions prospects appropriately
- Presents products on a problem-to-solution basis
- Continuously evaluates customer feedback and recommendations
- Delivers efficient service and high quality
- Possesses a detailed knowledge of formal agreements with vendors
- Effectively translates customer requirements to match our system
- Resolves inquiries regarding order status and general product information
- Regularly resolves billing errors via debit and credit memos
- Qualifies new customers in terms of systems ordering capability
- Rapidly investigates errant shipments and shortage inquiries
- Diagnoses the causes of problems and selects the best solutions

Needs Improvement

- Frequently fails to resolve customers' problems in a timely manner
- Does not proactively act on customers' suggestions
- Fails to bring problematic customer issues to management's attention
- Appears to cover up service issues rather than share them
- Does not submit product and service reports by established deadlines
- Demonstrates an insufficient knowledge of the online data entry system
- Commits excessive errors when documenting product numbers and change orders
- Sometimes fails to gain permission for approved or amended orders
- Lacks sufficient knowledge of updated products
- Continues to misdiagnosis basic customer inquiries
- Does not currently meet outbound call volume benchmarks
- Fails to qualify prospective customers
- Fails to ask questions that are critical to the sale
- Does not listen attentively to customers' needs

Executive Secretary

Meets/Exceeds Expectations

- Excels at providing one-on-one executive support
- Ensures that all aspects of office administration are well taken care of
- Independently composes correspondence without error
- Accurately takes dictation using shorthand/fast notes/ Dictaphone
- Requires little direction in completing administrative assignments
- Interfaces well with all levels of the senior management team
- Makes visitors feel comfortable and welcome in our office
- Is excellent resource on questions about office procedures and protocol
- Screens calls aggressively
- Is very protective of my time
- Is very attentive to detail when proofreading and editing drafts
- Ghostwrites memos for company-wide distribution
- Demonstrates good use of language and vocabulary
- Possesses advanced software skills
- Prepares sophisticated PowerPoint presentations for sales meetings
- Regularly attends meetings in my absence
- Finds creative ways to streamline the workflow
- Provides back-up administrative support to other members of management
- Always says yes to a request for help

✧ Is able to produce obscure or long-forgotten documentation quickly

Needs Improvement

✧ Has difficulty working for more than one boss
✧ Remains reluctant to say no when appropriate
✧ Fails to share what his other priorities are
✧ Does not regularly proofread or edit final drafts
✧ Commits too many grammar and spelling errors
✧ Fails to maintain an organized and up-to-date filing system
✧ Requires temporary back-up support too often
✧ Has difficulty managing my calendar and coordinating my travel schedule
✧ Demonstrates resistance when asked to answer others' phones
✧ Requires repeated instruction and close supervision

Facilities Maintenance Supervisor

Meets/Exceeds Expectations

✧ Supervises utility workers and contractors in general plant upkeep
✧ Regularly oversees the planning and design of buildings and other facilities
✧ Estimates costs for construction and facilities projects
✧ Coordinates the maintenance and remodeling of machinery
✧ Develops successful design criteria
✧ Serves as key point of contact with architectural and engineering firms
✧ Prepares accurate bid sheets
✧ Thoroughly inspects construction and installation progress
✧ Ensures conformance with established specifications and schedules
✧ Is knowledgeable of building code and regulatory compliance issues
✧ Effectively oversees clean-up, landscaping, and related work
✧ Provides guidance to mechanics, electricians, and contractors
✧ Troubleshoots repair issues for machines and equipment
✧ Maintains the computerized maintenance management system
✧ Acts as main contact for vendors on construction and deliveries

Needs Improvement

✧ Is technically lacking in the areas of electrical and plumbing

✧ Regularly neglects responsibilities for setup and take-down of equipment
✧ Fails to ensure that manpower and machines are available when needed
✧ Does not obtain sufficient price quotes for needed repairs
✧ Fails to communicate production challenges and delays

Office Manager

Meets/Exceeds Expectations

✧ Ensures the proper flow of work throughout the office
✧ Manages the dual role of supervising staff and maintaining office systems
✧ Ensures a high level of office staff performance
✧ Closely monitors her direct reports' efforts
✧ Forecasts the administrative and operational needs of the office
✧ Accurately schedules office expenditures
✧ Identifies and resolves budget variances
✧ Constructs action templates that others could follow in his absence
✧ Serves as jack of all trades
✧ Accurately maintains petty cash and stocks of office supplies
✧ Troubleshoots hardware and software problems
✧ Regularly prepares weekly attendance reports
✧ Processes payroll without error
✧ Administers equipment purchase, rental, and repair

Needs Improvement

✧ Has difficulty confronting subordinates' problematic performance
✧ Alienates other support staff members who do not report directly to her
✧ Clearly prefers the technical over the people-oriented aspects of her job

- ⟡ Lacks an advanced level of computer proficiency
- ⟡ Must rely on others to handle even the most basic of computer-related tasks
- ⟡ Is rarely willing to work overtime
- ⟡ Resists any change from established office guidelines
- ⟡ Shows favoritism to certain members of his team
- ⟡ Avoids mail sorting and distribution responsibilities
- ⟡ Resists dealing with the sudden changes to schedule
- ⟡ Fails to follow office policy and protocol

Receptionist

Meets/Exceeds Expectations

✧ Pleasantly greets, welcomes, and directs visitors
✧ Duly notifies employees of visitors' arrivals
✧ Generates a professional image of the company
✧ Serves as the first point of contact for all incoming phone calls
✧ Makes introductions in a professional and warm manner
✧ Serves as the first checkpoint of building security
✧ Ensures that all visitors have appropriate identification badges
✧ Voluntarily walks guests to their destinations rather than leaving them on their own
✧ Routes all departmental mail accurately
✧ Distributes all incoming courier packages to recipients in a timely manner
✧ Follows all front office policies and procedures
✧ Refers potential conflicts with visitors to the appropriate manager
✧ Receives recognition from visitors regarding her friendliness and professionalism
✧ Readily provides back-up support work without being asked

Needs Improvement

✧ Has difficulty directing callers to the appropriate parties
✧ Lacks familiarity with key players in the organization

- ❖ Fails to ensure that visitors sign the logbook and wear badges
- ❖ Leaves the desk too often to fraternize with others
- ❖ Permits an excessive number of incoming calls to go to voicemail
- ❖ Displays a lackluster and apathetic attitude
- ❖ Acts as if certain manual duties are below him
- ❖ Fails to follow front office dress code protocol
- ❖ Has not yet mastered the technical aspects of the telephone system
- ❖ Has particular difficulty coordinating conference calls
- ❖ Gets flustered when the console lights up with too many incoming calls
- ❖ Leaves callers on hold for excessive periods of time

Research Manager

Meets/Exceeds Expectations

❖ Successfully plans, executes, and analyzes traditional marketing research

❖ Effectively aids management decisions on new product/service development

❖ Continually evaluates the effectiveness of research

❖ Continuously investigates new research tools and methodologies

❖ Helps clients improve their strategic vision and profit

❖ Identifies new market trends and opportunities

❖ Strategically assesses market and competitive conditions

❖ Excels at managing qualitative and quantitative market research projects

❖ Supports new product development

❖ Regularly engages in data collection and research design

❖ Prepares effective survey instruments and discussion guides

❖ Is highly regarded for the quality of her research design and analysis

❖ Demonstrates solid report writing skills

❖ Proactively investigates new methods and technologies

❖ Regularly recommends testing and validation

❖ Delivers actionable marketing insights in a cost-effective manner

❖ Excels at assessing primary market research needs

Needs Improvement

❖ Has difficulty relating to consumer wants and needs

❖ Lacks a thorough understanding of marketing and customer profiling

- ❖ Remains challenged by proposal writing
- ❖ Has difficulty outlining objectives, methodologies, and costs
- ❖ Has yet to demonstrate full competency in research design and analysis
- ❖ Fails to consistently validate analyses against industry standards
- ❖ Has difficulty translating customer feedback into actionable recommendations
- ❖ Lacks familiarity with Nielsen syndicated data and statistical software

2

Risk Manager

Meets/Exceeds Expectations

✧ Effectively forecasts risks
✧ Designs, negotiates, and purchases appropriate insurance coverage
✧ Identifies all factors with the potential for causing financial losses
✧ Participates in the management of major claims
✧ Keeps management properly advised of pending risks
✧ Develops policies that prevent or mitigate loss exposures
✧ Develops insurance and risk management emergency response policies
✧ Strategically analyzes corporate insurance requirements
✧ Forecasts and budgets for insured and retained losses and premiums
✧ Effectively sets claim reserves
✧ Provides appropriate loss indemnification language for proposed contracts
✧ Collects, develops, and analyzes insurance underwriting information
✧ Manages compliance with state regulations and insurers' requirements
✧ Prepares the annual insurance budget

Needs Improvement

✧ Does not accurately forecast premiums or allocate reserve variances
✧ Fails to consistently follow up on audit and examination findings

- ✧ Has not kept abreast of recent changes in laws and applicable regulator guidance
- ✧ Has missed opportunities to review leases, contracts, and operational policies
- ✧ Lacks knowledge of workers' compensation and claims monitoring
- ✧ Has not yet learned how to measure and monitor credit exposures

Safety and Security Supervisor

Meets/Exceeds Expectations

❖ Successfully supervises a broad range of health and safety activities

❖ Demonstrates mastery of OSHA compliance and workers compensation

❖ Ensures compliance with all aspects of our safety and security program

❖ Leads business recovery, site security, and evacuation planning efforts

❖ Regularly conducts programs for the safety and security of employees

❖ Has developed a workable corporate disaster plan

❖ Carefully reviews injury and vehicle accident trends

❖ Readily recommends effective safety enhancements and corrective actions

❖ Maintains accurate records of inspections, periodic maintenance, and repairs

❖ Supervises inspections of fire suppression systems, extinguishers, and alarms

❖ Facilitates effective access control

❖ Ensures that ID badges, pass codes, and keys are in proper working order

❖ Regularly maintains security alarm authorized user lists and codes

❖ Serves as a single point of contact for all security system issues

❖ Conducts timely investigations of all work-related safety accidents

✧ Regularly accompanies all insurance inspectors on walk through tours

Needs Improvement

✧ Fails to maintain accurate records of inspections and audits
✧ Does not keep abreast of improvements in safety equipment
✧ Fails to conduct industrial hygiene surveillance inspections
✧ Does not regularly communicate safety and security concerns to management
✧ Has fallen behind in providing employee safety orientation training

Transportation Supervisor

Meets/Exceeds Expectations

- ✧ Schedules the timely delivery of freight
- ✧ Manages both the fleet and driver workforce
- ✧ Oversees the general supervision of transportation logistics
- ✧ Maintains the truck routing system and daily dispatch sheet
- ✧ Regularly identifies opportunities to increase back-haul revenue
- ✧ Communicates effectively with vendors, trucking companies, and buyers
- ✧ Regularly maintains dispatch schedules
- ✧ Ensures that loads are shipped on time
- ✧ Provides up-to-date information to drivers, clerks, and back-haul coordinators
- ✧ Creates timely tracking reports
- ✧ Effectively tracks goals, customer service, and cost control
- ✧ Coordinates efficient route deliveries
- ✧ Ensures timely pickup times for scheduled back hauls
- ✧ Ensures compliance with company policies and federal DOT regulations
- ✧ Prioritizes the flow of trucks and trailers

Needs Improvement

- ✧ Resents having to occasionally deliver product himself
- ✧ Fails to effectively coordinate dispatch functions and load efficiencies

- ❖ Often fails to ensure the timely departures of loads
- ❖ Does not sufficiently support hub operations
- ❖ Does not readjust for inbound/outbound schedules, delays, or re-routes
- ❖ Cannot yet demonstrate mastery of trucking software

Warehouse Manager

Meets/Exceeds Expectations

❖ Manages all aspects of warehouse operations
❖ Successfully oversees receiving, shipping, and cycle counting
❖ Plans, organizes, and monitors all activities within the receiving warehouse
❖ Ensures smooth and consistent warehouse operations
❖ Responsibly accounts for the accuracy of the warehouse inventory
❖ Ensures the timely flow of materials into and out of the warehouse
❖ Oversees the safe and efficient movement of incoming materials
❖ Regularly ensures that materials are stored properly to conserve space
❖ Has strong knowledge of warehouse and material handling operations
❖ Monitors uniform procedures for storing, inventorying, and shipping
❖ Successfully moves materials to and from storage configurations
❖ Generates up-to-date task lists, operating instructions, and error reports
❖ Insists on an orderly, clean, and accident-free department

Needs Improvement

❖ Fails to adequately manage the computerized inventory control program

- ✧ Does not consistently examine work for exactness or conformance to policy
- ✧ Neglects inspecting the physical condition of the warehouse and equipment
- ✧ Fails to maintain inventory accuracy of 97 percent or better
- ✧ Does not safely operate material handling equipment

Sales, Marketing, and Advertising

Account Executive

Meets/Exceeds Expectations

- ✧ Excels at identifying and closing new sales prospects
- ✧ Engages in a consultative selling style
- ✧ Continuously meets or exceeds sales expectations
- ✧ Generates a high number of leads through cold calling and personal referrals
- ✧ Sets the appropriate number of sales activities to meet performance targets
- ✧ Strategically conducts the appropriate needs analysis
- ✧ Presents products on a problem-to-solution basis
- ✧ Always puts the customer's needs above the need to close the sale
- ✧ Makes the greatest number of sales presentations month after month
- ✧ Tracks the quality ratios of sales calls to maximize each territory's potential
- ✧ Develops and follows a well-researched client development plan
- ✧ Remains in the top tenth percentile of account executives in terms of revenues

✧ Closes a high volume of new business and account renewals

✧ Sees each sale through to the client's satisfaction

✧ Maintains accurate records of cold calls, presentations, and sales results

✧ Readily handles contract renewals and price adjustments

✧ Proactively identifies current and future customer service requirements

✧ Quickly establishes rapport with potential customers

✧ Demonstrates effective negotiation and closing techniques

✧ Secures profitable, high margin business

✧ Maintains long-term client relationships

✧ Has a very high retention and repeat-business rating

Needs Improvement

✧ Is more transaction-oriented than relationship-driven

✧ Does not proactively identify and evaluate unexploited assets or revenue sources

✧ Has not consistently met monthly sales quotas

✧ Spends too much time chasing low margin business

✧ Has ongoing difficulties maintaining a stable portfolio of clients

✧ Shies away from negotiating complex deals

✧ Cannot effectively articulate competitors' strengths and weaknesses

✧ Is unable to articulate the company's competitive advantage

✧ Fails to pursue opportunities for account growth and new business development

✧ Has developed a reputation for being territorial and inflexible

❖ Fails to close major business deals within his assigned territory
❖ Has difficulty developing industry relationships and networks

Art Director

Meets/Exceeds Expectations

✦ Creatively conceptualizes and develops advertising campaigns

✦ Supervises the preparation and acquisition of all advertising materials

✦ Conceptualizes, develops, and executes key art

✦ Generates appropriate artwork and ancillary promotional materials

✦ Effectively designs all necessary advertising materials

✦ Directs the execution of key art

✦ Manages all aspects of illustration, retouching, and digital image creation

✦ Provides art direction and design supervision of final presentations

✦ Ensures timely and accurate cost estimates and financial accountability

✦ Successfully creates presentation boards to present to clients

✦ Develops art for trade print publications and point-of-purchase displays

Needs Improvement

✦ Lacks detailed knowledge of the creative tools available

✦ Designs concepts and layouts that are inconsistent with brand guidelines

✦ Does not stay current with the latest graphic trends

✦ Fails to meet advertising project deadlines and budgets

✦ Lacks experience in both design and illustration

✦ Lacks a functional knowledge of mechanical production

Cashier/Checker

Meets/Exceeds Expectations

✧ Accurately totals customers' purchases
✧ Itemizes payments at point of sale
✧ Displays a thorough knowledge of store products and merchandise
✧ Ensures proper cash register balancing with no variances
✧ Regularly verifies consumers' credit
✧ Encourages customers to purchase store credit cards
✧ Accurately enters price changes
✧ Ensures that price sheets and coupons are up to date
✧ Properly handles exchanges and returns merchandise
✧ Provides accurate pricing information
✧ Discounts purchases by redeeming coupons
✧ Readily alerts management to any potential security or theft violations

Needs Improvement

✧ Does not consistently demonstrate strong customer service skills
✧ Has difficulty balancing the cash drawer
✧ Fails to discount information that is not preprogrammed into the system
✧ Appears unwilling to perform noncashier duties, such as stocking and lifting
✧ Fails to proactively assist customers in locating merchandise

❖ Neglects keeping display tables well-stocked for convenient shopping
❖ Does not readily document out-of-stock merchandise
❖ Fails to consistently ensure that UPC codes on merchandise are correct

Event/Conference Coordinator

Meets/Exceeds Expectations

❖ Successfully processes seminar and convention registrations

❖ Accurately records payments for registrants, exhibitors, and sponsors

❖ Prepares name badges and event registration rosters without error

❖ Assists in managing the logistics of speaker presentations

❖ Diligently books guest and meeting rooms

❖ Ensures the timely distribution of promotional materials for seminars

❖ Coordinates the collection, compilation, and packaging of speakers' notes

❖ Assists in the management of volunteer corps

❖ Regularly maintains seminar, conference, and convention event schedules

❖ Distributes participant continuing education forms

❖ Obtains state licensing board CE credit approval for seminars

❖ Willingly assists in all levels of pre-conference planning

❖ Ensures that meeting rooms are properly equipped and prepared

❖ Coordinates all aspects of on-site signage and audiovisual requirements

Needs Improvement

❖ Fails to consistently coordinate catering and audiovisual requirements

- ✧ Lacks a basic knowledge of event and meeting planning principles
- ✧ Is slow to wrap up post-conference financial settlement of invoices
- ✧ Is not familiar with the operational requirements for audiovisual equipment
- ✧ At times appears resentful of early morning, evening, and weekend hours

Fundraising/Development Executive (Nonprofit)

Meets/Exceeds Expectations

✧ Responsibly oversees the planning and execution of all fundraising
✧ Manages the solicitation and stewardship of major gift prospects
✧ Devises strategies for achieving fundraising goals
✧ Develops contributed financial support, including membership and grants
✧ Serves as liaison with news media for exhibitions and special programs
✧ Demonstrates outstanding leadership working with boards of directors
✧ Skillfully organizes and coordinates social and special events
✧ Continuously solicits corporate underwriters and in-kind donations
✧ Diligently oversees annual membership drives
✧ Spearheads membership drives, including direct mail and telephone solicitations
✧ Instills trust and loyalty in clients and contributors
✧ Possesses solid experience in major gifts and planned giving

Needs Improvement

✧ Does not possess comprehensive fundraising or grant-writing skills
✧ Neglects the development of planned giving and endowment initiatives

❖ Lacks knowledge of intestacy laws and estate planning strategies
❖ Has difficulty structuring and conducting planned giving campaigns
❖ Is not familiar with credit trusts and wealth replacement trusts
❖ Has not consistently met fundraising and development target goals

Graphic Designer

Meets/Exceeds Expectations

✧ Provides graphic design and graphics production support
✧ Promptly completes layout revisions
✧ Optimizes and retouches graphics
✧ Creatively illustrates concepts
✧ Successfully designs rough layout of art and copy
✧ Has a good sense of appropriate graphic size, style, and arrangement
✧ Makes edits and changes to files in a timely and efficient manner
✧ Is flexible and willing to experiment with color, contrast, and backgrounds
✧ Develops new and exciting patterns and designs
✧ Successfully launches special design projects
✧ Implements art direction and design concepts across a range of projects
✧ Consistently verifies size, color, and other production-related issues
✧ Reliably executes graphic output for single-color and multicolor ads
✧ Processes form orders in accordance with eligibility guidelines

Needs Improvement

✧ Lacks necessary Web and HTML coding skills
✧ Is technically challenged in the areas of scanning and image production

- ❖ Fails to maintain graphic design equipment in proper working order
- ❖ Fails to regularly purge files of forms that are no longer in use
- ❖ Does an unsatisfactory job maintaining archival creative job files

Market Research Analyst

Meets/Exceeds Expectations

❖ Initiates marketing campaigns

❖ Does a thorough job identifying marketing opportunities

❖ Researches and analyzes market data

❖ Provides strategic decision support for marketing management

❖ Delivers relevant and accurate information, analysis, and insight

❖ Successfully analyzes and synthesizes survey data

❖ Prepares accurate reports of findings to marketing management

❖ Evaluates promotional materials

❖ Produces regular forecasts of market trends and competitive activity

❖ Works closely with internal customers to define initial requirements

❖ Tests products to make effective product recommendations

❖ Composes questionnaires and interprets results

❖ Develops trend data based on test panel results

❖ Performs campaign response analysis and modeling

❖ Provides insight into customer retention and cross-sell potential

❖ Regularly provides data-driven analysis of current marketing activities

❖ Identifies and extracts lists according to campaign specifications

Needs Improvement

- Fails to make clear recommendations based on research findings
- Lacks the ability to communicate technical results to non-technical audiences
- Makes ineffective recommendations regarding product positioning
- Relies too heavily on outside agencies
- Continues to exceed budget
- Lacks proficiency in direct marketing analytical methods
- Does not communicate effectively with sales and R&D staff

Marketing Director

Meets/Exceeds Expectations

✧ Effectively conceptualizes, develops, and executes marketing campaigns

✧ Successfully drives the creation and delivery of integrated marketing solutions

✧ Meets strategic marketing objectives

✧ Creates consistent campaigns across all marketing media

✧ Uses direct mail, e-mail blasts, and billboards to ensure maximum penetration

✧ Tailors marketing campaigns to promote products with the highest revenue potential

✧ Creates and develops collateral and brochures

✧ Ensures the accurate delivery of consolidated plans within allocated budgets

✧ Oversees all aspects of response tracking and measurement

✧ Excels at new account acquisition

✧ Successfully retains relationships with assigned/existing accounts

✧ Readily accepts the challenge of new sales activities

✧ Works well with the sales team in prospecting, qualifying, and closing sales

✧ Serves as an effective liaison between customers and our internal technical team

✧ Regularly ensures successful project completion and customer satisfaction

✧ Employs churn, satisfaction, and usage metrics for customer satisfaction programs

❖ Maintains dialog with account directors to up-sell additional functionality

Needs Improvement

❖ Fails to work closely with the installation team during implementation
❖ Misses opportunities to develop long-term relationships with key contacts
❖ Fails to review client accounts for up-sell or cross-sell opportunities
❖ Is unable to answer basic questions about sales projections
❖ Fails to create compelling and innovative marketing campaigns
❖ Lacks skills in the areas of online sweepstakes and product placement

Media Planner

Meets/Exceeds Expectations

✧ Effectively executes media campaigns

✧ Oversees the creation of media plan flowcharts

✧ Handles all buying, tracking, and reporting of media plans

✧ Develops and implements media objectives and strategies

✧ Takes charge of the creation and maintenance of media plans and budgets

✧ Efficiently tracks advertising spending by market

✧ Keeps up to date with the current media landscape

✧ Maintains professional relationships with the media community

✧ Regularly researches new opportunities with current and future clients

✧ Develops media objectives and strategies across all types of media

✧ Generates accurate tracking report evaluations

✧ Attends client meetings, prepares budgets, and generates competitive analyses

✧ Develops accurate specification sheets and requests for proposal

✧ Coordinates invoicing, quality control, and reconciliation of media buys

Needs Improvement

✧ Fails to analyze the value of media vehicles for client media plans

✧ Lacks sufficient quantitative skills to create formulas and execute calculations

- ❖ Neglects buying and trafficking responsibilities
- ❖ Fails to reconcile media buys and administer requests for proposal
- ❖ Lacks proficiency with syndicated research or media planning tools
- ❖ Fails to maintain deliverable schedules with all necessary changes and additions

Product/Brand Manager

Meets/Exceeds Expectations

✦ Develops key marketing and sales programs
✦ Ensures the appropriate implementation of marketing plans
✦ Has a keen understanding of marketing principles and practical applications
✦ Prepares and updates marketing budgets
✦ Accurately projects costs for all advertising and point-of-purchase materials
✦ Skillfully calculates budgets against projected revenues
✦ Develops point-of-purchase items, trade materials, and special promotions
✦ Effectively allocates marketing materials through all channels of distribution
✦ Analyzes the effectiveness of past promotions
✦ Incorporates successful elements of past promotions into future marketing plans
✦ Schedules releases and promotions that capitalize on market opportunities

Needs Improvement

✦ Does not expedite the approval of sales materials
✦ Fails to ensure that program releases are announced in a timely manner
✦ Fails to develop cross-promotional opportunities with outside companies
✦ Shows little effort to maximize product visibility and boost sales

❖ Provides minimum input regarding development of art materials and copy
❖ Does not adjust inventory levels and production schedules on a regular basis
❖ Fails to establish appropriate time schedules for bringing new product to market

Publicist

Meets/Exceeds Expectations

- ✤ Develops superior press materials and media lists
- ✤ Satisfies media requests
- ✤ Produces publicity materials that require little editing or correction
- ✤ Attentively oversees event planning and media relations
- ✤ Maintains comprehensive and current database of contacts
- ✤ Drafts company press releases and feature articles
- ✤ Plans, develops, and communicates relevant publicity information
- ✤ Keeps the public informed of clients' programs, accomplishments, and points of view
- ✤ Serves as a liaison with industry press to maximize publicity
- ✤ Diligently maintains the editorial calendar
- ✤ Cultivates rich stories for articles
- ✤ Successfully creates and distributes press kits
- ✤ Regularly attends industry trade shows and press conferences
- ✤ Promotes goodwill through publicity efforts
- ✤ Excels at organizing charitable events
- ✤ Prepares fact sheets, news releases, and photographs for media representatives

Needs Improvement

- ✤ Fails to sufficiently research and seek out new media outlets

- ❖ Misses opportunities to strengthen and develop media contacts
- ❖ Hesitates to participate in industry data-gathering surveys
- ❖ Fails to consistently capture and report publicity campaign results
- ❖ Does not take the initiative to independently research data
- ❖ Fails to proactively contact and court media representatives

Sales Assistant (Brokerage)

Meets/Exceeds Expectations

✧ Successfully provides sales and marketing support
✧ Skillfully handles unsolicited calls from prospects
✧ Consistently follows high standards of business and professional ethics
✧ Work well with high net worth individuals and institutional investors
✧ Coordinates a high volume of administrative support activities
✧ Qualifies new leads according to pre-established guidelines
✧ Successfully schedules appointments for call-ins with account executives
✧ Regularly follows up with referrals, prospects, and clients
✧ Distributes marketing brochures at the direction of sales representatives
✧ Ensures that corporate compliance standards are met
✧ Regularly records all transactions on appropriate logs and blotters
✧ Helps clients complete new accounts and asset transfers
✧ Efficiently handles routine matters, like address changes and bank authorizations
✧ Executes client trades accurately

Needs Improvement

✧ Lacks knowledge of securities industry terminology and practices

✧ Has difficulty preparing sales proposals due to limited software skills

✧ Fails to order and distribute client birthday and holiday cards

✧ Does not track and trend investment fluctuations and variations

✧ Fails to research and resolve client service problems in a timely fashion

✧ Fails to proactively notify sponsor companies when client problems arise

Sales Associate (Retail)

Meets/Exceeds Expectations

- Provides exceptional customer service
- Promotes retail sales and maximizes revenues
- Provides dedicated, one-on-one support to customers
- Possesses a creative flair for arranging products in an attractive manner
- Ensures that customers receive a distinctive brand experience
- Develops lasting customer relationships through clientele building practices
- Displays, promotes, tags, and prices merchandise as appropriate
- Prepares appropriate promotional signage
- Displays merchandise in accordance with company policy
- Excels in the areas of merchandising and visual presentation
- Ensures that operation standards and loss prevention guidelines are met
- Participates in continual sales and customer service training
- Consistently achieves customer satisfaction, sales standards, and goals
- Has developed a large base of repeat business
- Ensures consistent customer satisfaction
- Works flexible hours, even on last-minute notice, including weekends
- Shows a strong sense of integrity and commitment to customer satisfaction
- Accurately operates a retail computer point-of-sale system

- Maintains a working knowledge of service and repair operations
- Coordinates customer returns and exchanges according to store policy

Needs Improvement

- Does not display a positive and outgoing customer orientation
- Get easily overwhelmed during peak sales periods
- Fails to implement store merchandising standards
- Consistently forgets to take advantage of cross-selling opportunities
- Does not educate customers on related products, features, and services
- Has experienced difficulty in meeting and exceeding individual sales goals
- Is reluctant to work at multiple retail locations within the district, as required
- Fails to cultivate new customer relationships
- Does not regularly follow up with all customers after the sale
- Misses opportunities to obtain repeat sales

Sales Manager

Meets/Exceeds Expectations

✧ Effectively develops sales, marketing, and revenue plans

✧ Drives future growth and market share

✧ Drives incremental revenue

✧ Develops and executes a coherent business strategy

✧ Recommends short- and long-range business development objectives

✧ Successfully assesses trends, problems, and revenue opportunities

✧ Skillfully articulates the value of our products and services to customers

✧ Responds to questions in real-time

✧ Aggressively implements marketing strategies

✧ Motivates the sales staff

✧ Monitors sales staff performance

✧ Ensures that sales staff receives necessary training

✧ Forecasts and develops annual sales quotas

✧ Consistently projects expected sales volume and profitability

✧ Provides line organization input into pricing proposals

✧ Develops strategies and tactics for new business generation

✧ Coordinates business development and project management initiatives

✧ Regularly develops and introduces technical and management innovations

Needs Improvement

- Fails to develop successful sales plans
- Does not fully understand the economic metrics that drive the business
- Is uncomfortable with technology fundamentals
- Misses opportunities to build revenue through new partner acquisitions
- Shies away from structuring, negotiating, and closing complex deals
- Fails to build strategic partnerships
- Does not produce reliable and consistent business plans
- Is inconsistent in managing the performance of sales staff

Sales Representative (Outside)

Meets/Exceeds Expectations

❖ Diligently works an assigned territory to identify business opportunities

❖ Regularly meets with decision makers to analyze customers' requirements

❖ Consistently employs a consultative, customer-focused sales approach

❖ Excels at obtaining orders and establishing new accounts

❖ Readily recommends changes in products, service, and policy

❖ Makes compelling sales presentations

❖ Gains the attention and involvement of potential customers

❖ Establishes common ground and focuses on win-win outcomes

❖ Readily gains concessions and protects organizational interests

❖ Consistently closes the sale

❖ Addresses customer concerns and moves the customer toward commitment

❖ Skillfully uses territory analysis to target top prospects

❖ Consistently meets or exceeds sales targets

❖ Effectively uses cold calls and networking to generate new referrals

❖ Thoroughly qualifies leads

❖ Builds and maintains customer relationships long after the initial sale

❖ Provides the highest level of customer service support

❖ Uses collaborative selling strategies

✧ Identifies, cultivates, and leverages customer relationships
✧ Demonstrates expert negotiation techniques
✧ Possesses well-honed analytical skills to identify and exploit key opportunities
✧ Instinctively addresses customer concerns with savvy resolution strategies

Needs Improvement

✧ Does not consistently meet sales goals
✧ Lacks the business acumen to interpret financial information
✧ Has ongoing difficulties identifying client needs
✧ Lacks expertise in the techniques of collaborative selling
✧ Fails to spontaneously adjust the content or emphasis of sales presentations
✧ Gives up too easily when customers are resistant
✧ Does not retain clear records of submitted orders
✧ Frequently demonstrates resistance to travel throughout the sales territory

Telemarketer

Meets/Exceeds Expectations

✧ Generates a high volume of outbound telephone calls
✧ Renews a high percentage of extended warranty/service contracts
✧ Remains motivated and eager to cold call sales prospects
✧ Has a high ratio of sales closes per call
✧ Demonstrates thorough product knowledge
✧ Approaches contacts with a pleasant phone voice and gentle persistence
✧ Sells the sizzle when selling the steak
✧ Distinguishes between features and benefits
✧ Actively solicits orders for merchandise and services
✧ Consistently exceeds the required number of outbound telephone calls
✧ Records and secures information after each call
✧ Completes orders entries accurately

Needs Improvement

✧ Spends too much time with house accounts rather than new customers
✧ Frequently runs out of call contacts due to lack of daily preparation
✧ Has lower quality ratios than average
✧ Demonstrates reluctance to overcome initial customer objections
✧ Deviates too often from the script
✧ Overly apologies for the "intrusion" of his phone call

APPENDIXES

Appendix A:
High-Impact Verbs to
Inspire Your Writing

The *emphasized* verbs below may lend themselves to describing negative performance issues. Please review them whenever you have to address problematic performance in an appraisal.

A

Accepts
Acclimates
Accomplishes
Accounts (for)
Achieves
Acts (upon)
Adapts
Addresses
Adheres (to)
Adjusts
Administers
Adopts
Advances
Advises
Advocates
Aids
Aligns
Allocates
Allows
Amplifies
Analyzes
Anticipates
Applies
Appoints
Appraises
Appreciates
Approaches
Assembles
Assigns
Assumes (responsibility for)
Assures
Attends
Audits
Augments
Automates
Avoids

B

Balances
Broadens
Budgets
Builds

C

Capitalizes (on)
Captures
Challenges
Clarifies
Coaches
Collaborates (with)
Collects
Combines
Commits
Communicates
Compensates (for)
Compiles
Completes
Complies (with)
Composes
Comprehends
Compromises
Conceptualizes
Condenses
Connects (with)
Consolidates
Continues (to)
Contributes
Controls
Cooperates
Coordinates
Counsels

Creates
Cultivates
Customizes

D

Deals (with)
Debugs
Dedicates (him/herself to)
Defines
Delays
Delegates
Delivers
Demonstrates (mastery of)
Deploys
Designates
Designs
Detects
Determines
Develops
Deviates (from)
Devises
Devotes
Diagnoses
Differentiates (between)
Directs
Disburses
Disciplines
Discounts
Discourages
Dispatches
Displays
Disseminates
Distinguishes
Distributes

Documents
Dominates
Drafts
Draws (attention to)
Drives

E

Edits
Educates
Elicits
Eliminates
Embraces
Employs
Empowers
Enables
Encourages
Enforces
Engages
Engenders
Enhances
Enjoys
Ensures
Epitomizes
Escalates
Establishes
Estimates
Evaluates
Exceeds
Executes
Excels
Exercises
Exhibits
Expedites
Exploits

F

Facilitates
Fails (to)
Familiarizes (himself with)
Flags
Forecasts
Formulates
Fosters

G

Generates
Guides

H

Handles
Harbors
Heightens
Hesitates (to)
Highlights

I

Identifies
Implements
Improves
Incorporates
Increases
Informs
Initiates
Insists (on)
Inspires
Integrates
Institutes
Instructs

Interfaces (with)
Interprets
Investigates
Isolates
Issues
Itemizes

J

Justifies

K

Knows

L

Lacks
Leads
Lends
Leverages
Logs

M

Maintains
Makes (sure)
Manages
Masters
Maximizes
Minimizes
Models
Modifies
Monitors
Motivates

N

Navigates
Neglects
Negotiates
Notifies
Nurtures

O

Observes
Operates
Optimizes
Orchestrates
Organizes
Overcomes
Oversees
Overwhelms

P

Participates (in)
Plans
Prepares
Possesses
Postpones
Presents
Processes
Procrastinates
Produces
Progresses
Projects
Promotes
Protects
Provides

Publicizes
Purges

Q

Qualifies

R

Rationalizes
Recognizes
Recommends
Reconciles
Records
Redeems
Redirects
Reduces
Refers
Refines
Refrains (from)
Reinforces
Rejects
Rejuvenates
Renders
Reports
Represents
Requires
Researches
Resents
Resists
Resolves
Respects
Responds (to)
Retains
Rewards

Risks
Routes

S

Satisfies
Schedules
Secures
Seeks
Selects
Serves (as)
Shares
Shows
Simplifies
Solicits
Sources
Streamlines
Strengthens
Strives
Struggles (with)
Substantiates
Suffers (from)
Suggests
Summarizes
Supplies
Supports
Synchronizes
Synthesizes

T

Tailors
Targets
Thrives
Tolerates

Traces
Tracks
Transforms
Translates
Trends
Troubleshoots

U

Unites
Utilizes

V

Vacillates (between)
Validates
Verifies
Volunteers

W

Welcomes

Appendix B:
Essential Adverbs to Get
Your Message Across

The *emphasized* adverbs below may lend themselves to describing negative performance issues. Please review them whenever you have to address problematic performance in an appraisal.

A

Accurately
Actively
Adequately
Aggressively
Always
Appropriately
Assertively
Attentively

C

Carefully
Cautiously
Chiefly
Clearly
Cleverly
Closely

Collaboratively
Commonly
Completely
Comprehensively
Conscientiously
Consciously
Consecutively
Consistently
Constantly
Constructively
Continually
Continuously
Creatively

D

Deftly
Deliberately
Deservedly

Diligently
Directly
Duly

E

Effectively
Efficiently
Enthusiastically
Evidently
Excessively

F

Faithfully
Frequently
Fully

G

Generally

H

Habitually
Haphazardly

I

Inadvertently
Inappropriately
Inconsistently
Infrequently
Instinctively
Intentionally
Intermittently

K

Keenly
Knowingly

L

Largely
Logically

M

Masterfully
Methodically
Mistakenly
Mostly

N

Negatively
Never
Normally

O

Objectively
Occasionally
Often
Openly
Overly

P

Partially
Patiently
Periodically
Positively

Precisely
Predominantly
Proactively
Productively
Proficiently
Progressively
Promptly
Properly
Purposefully
Purposely

Q

Quickly

R

Rapidly
Rarely
Reactively
Readily
Regularly
Reliably
Reluctantly
Repeatedly
Respectfully
Responsibly
Rigidly
Routinely

S

Safely
Satisfactorily
Seldom
Sequentially

Skillfully
Smoothly
Sometimes
Specifically
Speedy
Spontaneously
Sporadically
Steadfastly
Steadily
Strategically
Strictly
Strongly
Subjectively
Substantially
Successfully
Succinctly
Suddenly
Swiftly
Systematically

T

Tactfully
Tactically
Thoroughly
Timely
Totally
Truly
Typically

U

Unexpectedly
Uniformly
Unintentionally

Appendix B

Unnecessarily
Usually

V

Vigorously
Voluntarily

W

Willfully
Willingly
Wisely

Appendix C:
Common Grading Scale

Although ranking systems differ from company to company, this common five-point scale will provide you with a consistent point of reference when rank-ordering your staff and determining overall performance scores:

5   Clearly outstanding
4   Consistently exceeds standards and expectations
3   Consistently meets standards and expectations
2   Needs improvement
1   Unacceptable / Unsatisfactory

Merit (salary) increases are typically awarded for individuals who receive overall scores of 3, 4, and 5. Merit increases are denied employees who receive overall scores of 1. Workers who receive an overall score of 2 may be granted another review at a later time (e.g., ninety days later) or be given a very low percentage increase (e.g., 1 percent). However, this may be subject debate depending on company policy and practice. After all, it could be seen as contradictory to award *any* salary increase to an employee who receives an overall score of 2. When in doubt, always check with qualified legal counsel in your state for a fact-specific analysis and recommendation.

Appendix D:
Index of Particular Titles and Roles

Learn More About Additional Titles from AMACOM at www.amacombooks.org: